Franco Cardini

TUSCANY

SCALA

distributed by Harper & Row, Publishers

CONTENTS

* * *

© Copyright 1986 by SCALA, Istituto Fotografico Editoriale,
Antella, Florence
Design: Ilaria Casalino and Fried Rosenstock
Translation: Patrick Creagh
Production: SCALA
Photographs: SCALA (M. Falsini, N. Grifoni, M. Sarri) except: nos. *4,
135* (Martin Streitenberger); *11, 12, 15, 18, 19, 20, 26, 33, 39, 89, 90,
94, 95, 102, 121, 158, 162, 163*, page 71/II, page 120/II (Nicola
Ricci); *100* (Federico Vianello); *101* (Verole Bozzello).
Printed in Italy by Lito Terrazzi, Cascine del Riccio, Florence

INTRODUCTION
THE NAME AND THE TERRITORY

When we speak of Tuscany we must first of all understand what we are talking about: a certain area with certain boundaries, an historical region the confines of which may coincide with those of the present political and administrative Region, though not entirely and not necessarily. All the same, we would be doing an injustice to its landscape, to its people, to its various modes of speech, to the traditions still flourishing there, if our appreciation of the basic unity within the region did not also do justice to the profound differences, the particulars, and in short all the very diverse, though harmonizing, voices that go to make up the chorus.

We often say "Tuscany" while thinking simply of Florence. It is for the most part non-Tuscans who fall into this trap, to the great indignation of the Tuscans (Florentines included), since the historical, linguistic and cultural structure of the region — in spite of the exceptional importance of the "capital," which in any case exceeds the confines of the region itself — is eminently polycentric. Someone attempted to define it, rather delightfully, as a "thousand-year-old city-culture." Yet even today, in the era of the megalopolis, between the folds of its hills and mountains, and on the carpets of its few restricted plains, this region of cities still preserves broad areas that are entirely or prevalently rural, or even uninhabited. It is often said that the Tuscans are absolutely unmistakable amongst the Italians, but by so saying we underestimate the fact that the region has many "frontier" areas, where this uniqueness is toned down, and where a Tuscan takes on something of Liguria, Emilia, Romagna, Umbria or Lazio.

The region contains a wealth of small differences, and even more or less evident internal divisions. From the basic point of view of climate, altitude and economy, there are in fact at least three Tuscanys: the region of the Appennines; the hilly areas which, from the rolling country of the "Lucchesia" across the gentle hills of Chianti and the Val d'Elsa, extend as far as the Colline Metallifere and Monte Amiata; and finally the coastal areas and the narrow river valleys wedged between hills and mountains. And this apart from the Tuscan islands, similar only in part to the coastal areas.

But the region also changes a great deal from north to south. To the north of the Arno, where Tuscany starts to climb into the Appennines, which press it closer and closer to the sea as one goes northwards, approaching Liguria and Emilia, the characteristics of the region are attenuated, and we have what we might call a "less Tuscan Tuscany." From the southern bank of the great river, almost as far as the gates of Siena, we find what may be the most specific and characteristic nucleus of the region (but to which, we repeat, the region itself cannot be entirely reduced, except at the price of unacceptable distortions). From Siena down we have the "Deep South" of Tuscany, with its treeless

1. *Landscape near San Quirico d'Orcia.*

2. *The island of Elba seen from the Gulf of Baratti.*

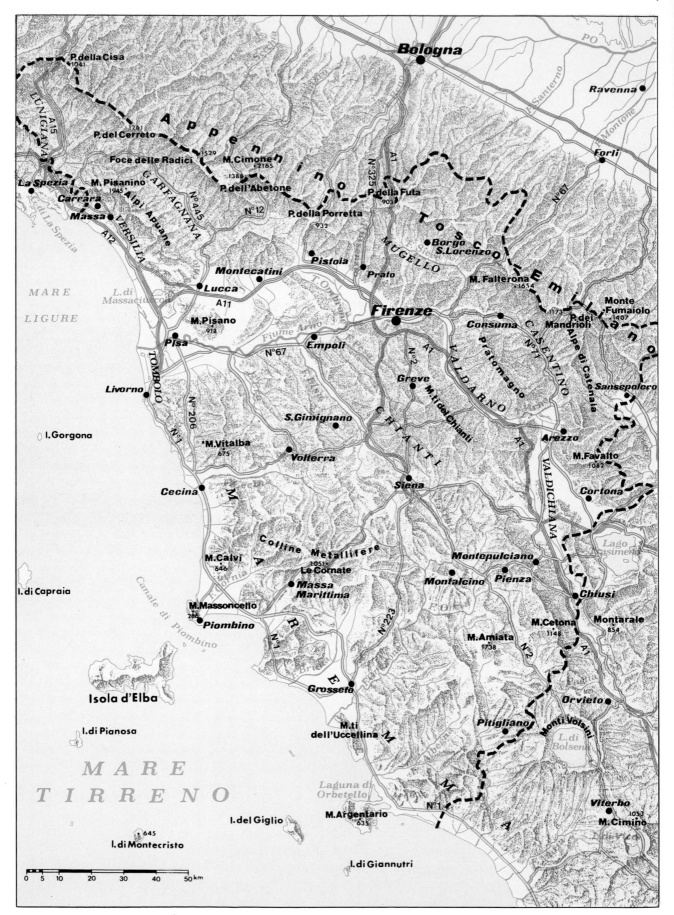

3

4

miles, with its Maremma, its sparser population, its different human and agricultural landscape.

Our Tuscany — the Tuscany we are about to speak of in these pages — is by no means a kind of magic triangle neatly outlined between the mountains and the Tyrrhenian Sea, clearly and precisely cut off from the rest of Italy. On the contrary, in one respect it is inextricably linked to the neighbouring regions, while in another it has within it so many diversities and nuances that any theory prejudicially in favour of unity would not hold water.

Ought one then to speak of "le Toscane," as we speak of "le Marche," "gli Abruzzi," and as until a short while ago we used to speak of "le Puglie" and "le Calabrie"? Well, no. And this denial is by no means emotional, but based on at least three valid reasons, one geographical, one historical, and the third linguistic and cultural. Geographically speaking the lines drawn by the Tyrrhenian, the Appennines and the Tiber mark out a pretty clear border, even if it is anything but "closed." Historically, after the organization provided by the Romans for the *"regio"* of Tuscia-Etruria, and the Late Mediaeval rise of a Longobard duchy (later a Frankish "march") of Tuscia, the leadership assumed by Florence in the process of transformation from a Commune to a regional State in the 14th and 15th century (in spite of considerable resistance from Siena and Lucca), and the establishment of the Grand Duchy under the houses of Medici and Lorraine, impressed an indelible stamp upon the region. Finally, Tuscan speech, in all its many varieties, has from the 13th century onwards, and in particular during the 19th century, asserted itself as the literary language of United Italy, while even for this very reason confirming its original character as a regional tongue. This last aspect of the matter is the very one which makes it difficult to talk about Tuscany to Italians other than Tuscans; on account of a linguistic and literary involvement, it is hard for any Italian today not to think of Tuscany as just a little bit his own. It is hard, that is, to think of it as a "foreign" region.

Having said this, we must add that this very feeling can give

3. Landscape with olive trees and vine-yards in the Chianti, between Florence and Siena. In the background, the parish church of San Donato in Poggio.

4. The woods of Vallombrosa.

5. The forest near the monastery of Ca-maldoli.

rise to the most dangerous misunderstandings, for beneath a surface that is clear, simple, rational, serene and polished, the Tuscan landscape and people can occasionally be intractable, harsh, closed and mysterious. It is no coincidence that the peoples who left the deepest marks on the region (although, in part, the least visible), and who made the greatest contribution to its unitary character, were two enigmatic and defeated peoples, two protagonists of vanished civilizations: the Etruscans and the Longobards.

The similarity between the Etruscans and the Longobards, historically rather implausible, nevertheless comes spontaneously to mind whenever we compare their histories to those of their respective victors, who in both cases brought with them a supra-regional and supra-national culture that was destined to found empires: the Romans and the Franks. In comparison with their hierarchical, co-ordinating and "vertical" spirit, both the Etruscans and the Longobards appear to have been endowed with a quite different genius. Though destined to lose out in immediate historical circumstances, it was based on local liberties and federal ties, and in short on "horizontal" relationships. The antipathy shown by the Tuscans, from the 14th century onwards, towards the growing dominance of Florence, may be explained not only by the rivalry between cities and parties typical of the era of the Communes during the Middle Ages, but also perhaps by this ancient tendency towards a federal equilibrium that did not tolerate dominant powers. From the Etruscan *poleis* to the mediaeval Communes there runs the golden thread of a preference for a "little homeland" and for an independence that is almost never chauvinistic or exclusive, but rather (except for times of bitter conflict, which there certainly were) inclined naturally towards alliance and exchange with the neighbouring "little homelands." Meanwhile within any type of settlement or small area, there grew up a multiplicity of local characteristics, with their various traditions, and maybe even rivalries, pride and obstinacies.

Many cities, historically hostile to one another; a changing, irregular landscape marked by ranges of hills and no lack of really mountainous areas; many valleys, usually narrow, and frequently only in quite recent times reclaimed from the marshes. If this lie of the land, everywhere uneven and at times rugged, may at least in part be the cause of the closed, argumentative and aggressive character of many of the Tuscan peoples, or at least of that rather pleasing roughness that is the basis of their common character, we should certainly add that a close look at its geological-historical features forces us to identify a number of sub-regional areas, each endowed with a robust character of its own.

With a few exceptions these areas correspond to the valleys of the most important rivers which cut through Tuscany. To start from the north-west of the region as defined for administrative purposes today, we first meet the basin of the river Magra, occupying the province of Massa-Carrara, which historically speaking looks towards Liguria, and was only assigned to Tuscany in 1871. This is the Lunigiana, the territory of the ancient city and diocese of Luni. Immediately to the south-east is the Garfagnana, which is the narrow valley of the river Serchio between the Apuan Alps and the watershed formed by the Appennines. To the south-west, there is the somewhat flat, sandy coastal area of the Versilia, with its pinewoods and its beaches, once fashionable and to some extent still so. With its centre at Viareggio, historically speaking this area is linked to one of the three great "capitals" of the region, Lucca. This same city is the centre for the lower valley of the Serchio — the Lucchesia — and the Valdinievole which includes the towns of Pescia and Collodi. Between Lucca and Pistoia the horizon is without any outstanding features until we get to Monte Albano and the middle Arno valley. This was a vast marshy area until it was reclaimed in the 18th century by order of the Grand Duke Pietro Leopoldo. From it emerge only the "islands" formed by small hills such as that of Montecatini Alto. Further north the landscape once more becomes rugged, with the mountains towering above Pistoia (Montagna Pistoiese) which act as the watershed between this territory and that of Bologna. Travelling eastwards, after the narrow Val di Bisenzio, we enter the valley of the Sieve and its tributaries, corresponding to the historical area of the Mugello. From here, once we cross the Futa Pass, 930 metres up in the Appennines, we leave the geographical but not the historical area of Tuscany. We have in fact arrived in "Tosco-Romagna," occupying the upper basins of the Santerno, the Senio and the Lamone, with their chief centres at Firenzuola, Palazzuolo sul Senio and Marradi. If to the north the Mugello crosses the Appennines into Romagna, to the south it shades off into the lower Val di Sieve. Here it meets the mid-valley of the Arno (Medio Valdarno) at Pontassieve, which stands at the meeting of the waters.

Pontassieve is in fact a key-point. The Arno, which begins life by flowing south, having rounded the massif of the Pratomagno turns sharply north, and makes a broad curve just before Pontassieve. Here it collects the tributary waters from the Mugello, and heads westward past Empoli to Pisa and the sea. From Pontassieve we can cross the wooded bulk of the Pratomagno by way of the Passo della Consuma and thereby reach the Casentino. This is the upper valley of the Arno, marked at its northernmost limits by the mountains of Falterona and Fumaiolo, the sources respectively of the Arno and the Tiber. Immediately east of the Casentino we come to the Val Tiberina, which borders on Umbria, as in fact does the Valdichiana, the neighbouring basin of the river Chiana.

But let us return to the Arno and look at the area to the south of its left bank. Between Pisa and the river Cècina the coast around Livorno towers high above the sea. This little river rises in the Colline Metallifere, and abounds in echoes of Etruscan culture. It flows into the sea almost as soon as it has passed the small town that is called after it, and to the south of this the coast once again becomes sandy and low-lying. This is the Maremma, the ancient *Maritima* now almost completely reclaimed, though it has not yet entirely lost the wonder of its great pinewoods, its

6

7

6. *Erosion furrows in the Valdarno, near Incisa.*

7. *The lake of Burano in Maremma, now a national park.*

8

9

8. *The valley of Acqua Cheta (still waters) and the Muraglione Pass in the Appennines.*

9. *Landscape near Volterra.*

pasturelands, its marshes abounding in wildfowl. The Maremma is divided into three parts: the "pisana" (between Cècina and the estuary of the Cornia), the "grossetana" (the coast between Cornia, Albegna and the lower reaches of the Ombrone), and the "senese" (upper reaches of the Ombrone), but it also extends as far as Monte Amiata, the Val d'Orcia, the Colline Metallifere and the so-called "Crete" (the bare, clay landscape south of Siena).

In the mid-valley of the Arno, between Empoli and San Miniato, we turn south into the broadest and most interesting valley in central Tuscany, the Val d'Elsa, along which ran the famous mediaeval road, the Via Francigena. From this valley to the south-west we may cross the hills around Volterra and reach the Val di Cècina and the sea. Going eastward we pass through the Chianti hills on our way to the upper Arno Valley with its chief centres at San Giovanni and Terranuova.

So here we have mountains, hills, valleys, marshes; woods of oak, chestnut and beech, with firs in the Appennines and vast pinewoods along the seashores; traces of a volcanic past visible here and there throughout the region, from Monte Morello to Monte Amiata, and which particularly in the centre and south of the region explain the presence of thermal springs of some importance; considerable deposits of metal ore, especially in the triangle between Massa Marittima, Amiata and the island of Elba; areas such as the middle and lower Arno valley, in which a vast population growth linked with an often unharmonious industrial development appear to have forever ruined the landscape and the balance of the environment, cheek by jowl with areas of apparently incontaminated beauty. These are the contradictions and contrasts which make Tuscany so full of surprises, and at the same time an explosive mixture of problems.

"THE MOST TOUCHING LANDSCAPE IN THE WORLD"

10. *Sheep grazing near San Gimignano.*

As we drive along the Autostrada del Sole, or else the hair-raising but nonetheless picturesque Via Aurelia, in spite of a wealth of wonderful glimpses and sudden, breathtaking sights, we may not always be aware that we are passing through what Fernand Braudel thought was "the most touching landscape in the world." If it is true that the Maremma ought to be seen in the scorching midsummer sun, and Chianti when the first vine-leaves begin to redden; and if the forest of Camaldoli is at its most bewitching in the early-morning mists, and the "Balza" at Volterra in the sunset, it stands to reason that we cannot always be at the right place at the right time of day or season of the year. All the same, the reputation for being "modern" and "dynamic" which Tuscany enjoys (and, let it be said, with ample justification) should not lead us to forget that it is one of the most densely wooded regions in the whole of Italy, and that it can boast a coastline 300 kilometers long.

Woods and sea shores, moreover, subject to decay and exposed to ecological death. From the outskirts of the Megalopolis that now stretches from Florence to Prato and Pistoia, and from Pisa to Livorno, or from the desolate stretches of the Appennines and the Garfagnana where emigration and the decline of population have created scores of abandoned villages, the traces of the landscape that inspired Benozzo Gozzoli, Leonardo and (later) Fattori are not always very clearly discernible. Tourism itself is a notorious factor in the ruin of the environment, and yet (this appears paradoxical only at first sight) it constitutes one of the strongest reasons for arresting this ruination, while at the same time proving that so far it has not succeeded in despoiling Tuscany of its fame not only as a land of art and culture, but also of unique "natural" beauties.

The adjective "natural" is a magical one; so why do I provoke the reader by putting it in inverted commas? History can perhaps suggest an answer, for when it comes down to it almost no landscape is natural. If the Tuscan landscape is really as "touching" as Braudel would have us believe, the fact is that such feeling never arises spontaneously and without reflection. Both landscape and feeling are the products of centuries of cultural evolution, of choices made, of co-existence between man and his environment.

Bulldozers and avalanches of cement, acres of rubble and of rubbish and the smoking factory-chimneys, all these change the face of city and country alike, and blur their colours. Yet, together with historical memory there is a geographical memory which resides in place-names and takes us back to a quite different set of images, to the landscape as it once was. Examples are the names of places in which we find such elements as "bosco" (wood), "macchia" (thicket), "prato" (meadow) — and the reader will have no difficulty in thinking of countless equivalents in English. Any territory is in fact a palimpsest. Nothing in it is really and truly

11

12

11. *View of the landscape near Castellina (Pisa).*

12. *Peasant house and tilled fields near Casciana Terme (Pisa).*

"natural," unless we are content with an Arcadian and properly speaking phoney concept of nature; nothing is really in an aboriginal state.

By the beginning of the first millennium B.C. the region had more or less taken on the appearance it has today, at least on the level of large-scale morphology. Lakes and marshes had already shrunk back from the plains, with the exception of the large basins of the lower Valdarno, the Maremma and the Valdichiana, while the volcanoes in the southern parts of the area — including Monte Amiata — were already extinct. Only the coastline, due to the constant accumulation of alluvial soil at the estuaries of the rivers, had a different profile, though not as different as all that. By the 7th to 6th centuries B.C. the sand-bars now forming the lagoon of Orbetello had already joined the Argentario to the mainland, while it was during those same centuries that Greek influence introduced both the vine and the olive. These two "timeless" spirits at work in the magic landscape of Tuscany are actually not timeless at all. There was, believe it or not, a time when wine and oil did not yet gladden the tables of our forebears (unless, of course, they were imported. . .). The cypress-tree, which only in this part of the world succeeds in being something other than a *memento mori*, was introduced here only in Etruscan-Roman times, when the reorganization of the network of roads and a new measurement and distribution of territory (known as "centuriation") gave the region a really new look. But we have to wait for the late Middle Ages and the dawn of the modern era before seeing the Tuscan landscape take on that unique balance between man and nature in which man lives in scattered farms covering the hills as if with a network of dwellings, close enough to each other but not too close. One might call it the ideal osmosis between a town immersed in nature's verdure and a densely populated countryside.

This admittedly is true above all in the upper Valdarno, in Chianti and in Val d'Elsa, areas often taken as the one and only model of the "Tuscan countryside," which in fact also has its share of harshness and desolation. Both the harmoniousness, which is largely one of yesterday's myths, and the pollution which is widespread though not total, must come to terms with the dynamics of history. This is true also of the climate, which changes like everything else in the process of time, and here as elsewhere is affected by the cutting down of the woods, and changes in the flow of water, and the general pollution of the environment. On the whole we now have a temperate Mediterranean climate, with the highest mean annual temperature in the Maremma (16° C) and the lowest in the valleys of the Appennines (12° C). Winters are often visited by the sun, but can also be fairly severe (especially when the northern "tramontana" wind blows), with a certain amount of snow, though (except in high mountain areas) fitful and seldom very deep. These alternate with a spring and autumn that are mild, though (especially spring) often rainy. The fact that the Apuan Alps are so close to the sea, and that therefore the warm sea-winds come up against an immediate obstacle, makes

13

14

Versilia an area of frequent rainfall. The coasts are also exposed to strong south-westerly gales, while the mid-August storms — to be feared the whole length of the coastline — disrupt the bathers on the beach in a way that has practically become a local tradition.

In geological terms the region of Tuscany is not all that ancient, and for the most part it cannot be placed earlier than the Tertiary Age. A metamorphosis taking place in the Tertiary Age does appear, in point of fact, to have produced the particularly crystalline quality of the marble from the Apuan Alps, while another example of prized marble is that of the so-called "Giallo di Siena," which comes from the Montagnola district. However, the most widespread stone in Tuscany is without doubt what is known as "macigno," a quartzose sandstone, while in the Apuan Alps and the Garfagnana a vast karstic area gives rise to numerous caves abounding in remains of palaeontological and prehistoric times. Geothermic phenomena in the region are many and various, and thermal baths are to be found all over the region, from the Lucchesia to the Sienese Maremma, as well as unusual phenomena such as the jets of hot air (known as "soffioni") in the region between the Cècina and the Cornia; discharges of gas (carbon dioxide, hydrogen sulphide), and the springs of hot water frequent in the territory of Lucca and of Siena.

With respect to its hills and mountains, everyone agrees that the first thing that strikes one about the beauty of Tuscany is its variety. By this we mean the abundance of high ground, summits and crests arranged in no apparent order, with a prevalence of hilly or very hilly country, mountains which occasionally rise to about 2000 metres (well over 6000 ft.) but are generally far more modest, and plains along the rivers and near the coast, which cover a bare 10% of the total area of the region. In the Garfagnana, the Appennines and the Alpi Apuane, the mountains can even resemble the Dolomites, and indeed they might be thought of as the "Tuscan Alps." Further south we find the beginnings of the central Italian Appennines, which are calcareous, usually bare, and rounded in outline. Between this range and the

13. Benozzo Gozzoli: Adoration of the Magi, detail of the landscape. Florence, Palazzo Medici Riccardi.

14. The hillside of Fiesole.

15

15. *A pasture in Garfagnana, near the peak of Pania Secca.*

coast is a series of irregularly alligned ridges, usually between 600 and 1000 metres in height (say, 2-3 thousand feet), stretching north-east and south-west between Montecatini and Monte Amiata. This is the so-called Antiappennino, in the centre of which is the system usually known as the Colline Metallifere. The plains, other than those along the coast, occupy the basins of the rivers Arno, Chiana and Tiber.

In view of the usual ratio between plains and river basins, it is not surprising that a region with so little flat land is endowed with a rather modest network of rivers. Given both the moderate rainfall and the prevalence of impermeable soils, even the major water-courses have a meagre flow, and even this is very seasonal (an exception is the Serchio, which rises in the high Appennines south of the Cisa Pass, in an area with heavy rainfall and permeable limestone soils). Though liable to both drought and flood (as we saw during the great flood of 1966), the Arno with its 241 kilometers in length and its tributaries from the left (Chiana, Pesa, Elsa, Era) and from the right (Sieve, Bisenzio) is the most impressive river in the region. Next comes the Ombrone (161 km.), with its tributary the Orcia, then the Serchio (103 km.). Following these, from north to south, are the Magra (65 km.), the Cècina (76 km.), the Cornia (50 km.), the Albegna (67 km.) and the Fiora (71 km.).

There once existed an extensive and intriguing Tuscany of lakes and marshlands. Between Florence, Pistoia and Lucca was the kingdom of the canebrakes, flat-bottomed barges and wildfowl, while the Valdichiana was a vast, shallow lake. The "Loggia del Pesce" which makes a fine, but faintly absurd, display of itself in the middle of Cortona — within sight of a Lake Trasimeno that has been irreversibly polluted — is a reminder of the times when lake-fish were abundant. The marshes provided Tuscans with their Lenten fare and plenty of game for their feast-days. Of all this, there is little left today: the lake of Massaciuccoli near Viareggio, with an area of some 7 square kilometers, the small marshes at Bientina and Fucecchio, the lakes of Montepulciano and Chiusi, as well as the coastal lake of Burano south of Orbetello. The little lakes in the Appennines are nothing but picturesque puddles. In exchange, we have a number of artificial lakes.

The islands of Tuscany, almost all of them within the stretch of sea between the promontory of Piombino and the Argentario (the exception being the more northerly Gorgona), are perhaps to be considered as an extension of the Antiappennines. They could well be the remains of the ancient land of *Tyrrhenis*, now long submerged, to which the Argentario itself belonged. The largest of the islands is Elba, which rises at its western end to over 1000 metres. Its iron deposits have been exploited since Etruscan times, while its rocky coasts — like those of the more southerly island of Giglio — are ideal for underwater fishing. We should also mention the craggy island of Montecristo, a granite rock now wisely protected as a reserve for flora and fauna, and the islet of Giannutri, with its ruined Roman villa.

Tuscany is not a bad place to go on a safari, at least if you are

16

a palaeontologist. If we may judge from the remains, found mostly in the upper Valdarno, the region once abounded in elephant, hippopotamus, rhinoceros, antelope, deer and several kinds of large felines. What we have today is less exotic, but not without interest, with roe-deer and (above all) wild boar in the Maremma; red and fallow deer and — in the forest of Campigna — even the mouflon or wild sheep, all these protected in the reserves of San Rossore, Migliarino and Alberese; badgers, foxes, porcupines and small carnivores (martens, polecats, otters) scattered all over the region. Bears, alas, disappeared about two hundred years ago, though in wintertime the occasional frightened wolf-cub may be glimpsed, on a visit from the Pratomagno or the Umbrian Appennines. To speak of birds, apart from the eagles which nest in the awe-inspiring scenery of the Orrido di Botri, in the Garfagnana, the most common denizen of the "maquis" is the partridge, whereas the pheasant is by now a mere mouthful for the dinner-table produced in the game reserves. Wild geese, mallard, snipe and coots are to be found at Massaciuccoli and in the little that is left of the marshes in Maremma. Amongst reptiles, apart from the many kinds of snake, a special interest is attached to a species of lizard that are widespread in the islands and on the Argentario, but not on the mainland. This we may consider evidence in favour of the existence of the ancient land of *Tyrrhenis*.

From the point of view of the flora, in common with the rest of a country with such a long coastline as Italy, the most obvious thing is the difference between the coastal area, where the "*Mediterranean maquis*" is predominant, and the interior with its vegetation more typical of the Appennines. The coastal "*maquis*" is a mixture (often very dense) of arbutus, holm-oak, myrtle, juniper and brambles. Man has in many instances replaced this wilderness with the pinetree, but in the last few decades forest fires both great and small, recurring every summer and in many cases almost certainly the result of arson, have once again changed the look of the coastal areas.

The moment we leave the coast the scene becomes what

17

16. *Ambrogio Lorenzetti: The Effects of Good Government in the Country, detail. Siena, Palazzo Pubblico.*

17 *The hills near Volterra.*

18

18. Portoferraio, on the island of Elba.

botanists describe as sub-Mediterranean, with small oak-trees, heather, juniper and a few patches of pines resulting from recent reforestation schemes. Between 300 and 600 metres this sub-Mediterranean flora gives place to mountain flora, and the scene is dominated by the chestnut up to heights of 800-1000 metres, above which is the kingdom of the beechtree.

Higher still the beech yields pride of place to the silver fir, which raises its stately head in the national forests of Abetone, of Vallombrosa and of Camaldoli. As the Appennines at this point are not all that lofty, there are relatively few and restricted areas totally free of trees and therefore devoted to pasture. The fact is that cattle-rearing in Tuscany does not amount to much. The situation is different for sheep and goats, which are increasingly occupying the areas abandoned by the shrinking cultivation of the hilly areas, turning what once were fields into grazing lands. In the Maremma an effort has been made to increase the population not only of horses but of buffalo. The latter are few and extremely costly, but with the help of ecology, *"agritourism"* and the present resurgent interest in these large, handsome beasts deserving to be saved from extinction, their numbers might possibly grow. In the summertime, around Punta Ala, you find a crowd of "dude" cowboys. They might make one scratch one's head from an anthropological point of view, but they also serve their purpose in the context of an "educated" type of tourism aware of the need to safeguard nature.

THE PEOPLE

An area of many populous cities, as well as a densely settled countryside, Tuscany has probably "always" been fairly well-populated, at least in historical times. All the same, we have nothing certain or reliable before the 14th-15th centuries, when surveys and land-registries provide us with a certain amount of information, in quantity if not in quality. It is hard to calculate the drop in population that doubtless struck the entire region in the first half of the 14th century, reaching its climax in the wake of the Black Death. After this the population began to grow again, interrupted only by a single (and far less serious) disaster with the plague of 1630. In the 16th century the Tuscans numbered about a million, and at the end of the 18th century about 1,200,000. In the 1860s (at the time of the unification of Italy) the number had grown to 2 million, and thence to about 3,600,000 according to the census of 1980. In recent years, with the rather drastic fall in the birth-rate and the number of marriages, population-growth has been at zero, or in fact slightly above that level owing to the influx of workers (chiefly from southern Italy) into the larger towns. Numerically far less important, there has also been a valuable immigration of Sardinian shepherds, who have brought their skills to large areas of the provinces of Siena and Grosseto. In comparison with immigrants entering Tuscany, the Tuscans who leave their homeland are relatively few. If anything they leave their birthplace but stay in the region, though this phenomenon is nothing new. There has been an exodus from mountainous and other isolated districts towards more developed and populated areas, such as the lower Valdarno, and of course towards the big towns in general. This is naturally quite a different matter from temporary "emigration" such as was involved in moving flocks of sheep between the Appennines and the Maremma, or that of woodsmen or charcoal-burners down into the Maremma. It was not until the early years of this century, immediately before the First World War, that there was any conspicuous emigration from Tuscany (and even then mostly from the Lucchesia, the Lunigiana and the Garfagnana) to foreign countries, including (for example) the United States.

The density of population is greatest in the lower Valdarno and the areas of Pisa, Livorno, and the southern district of Pistoia, and is sparser in Siena and Arezzo and above all in the vast province of Grosseto, where there are scarcely more than 200,000 inhabitants in an area of almost 4,500 square kilometers, which means less than 50 inhabitants per square kilometer. The regional average of roughly 150 inhabitants per square kilometer is some 20% lower than the Italian national average. But these are merely a few statistics, quoted in round numbers so as to give some idea of the scale of certain phenomena. But, given the profound historical and geographical differences obtaining between the various zones of Tuscany, the "regional average" in itself means little or nothing. Far more important, and perhaps more serious

19

19. The abandoned village of Campocatino (Lucca).

20

20. *The town of Guadine (Massa) on the Apuan Alps, a quarrier's village.*

in every way, is the tendency for the population to concentrate in certain areas. In the last few decades this has led to the annihilation of whole communities, especially in mountain areas, which have been replaced with "dormitory-towns" and the like, where relationships between individuals and different communities becomes a real problem. Let it be understood that this is true only up to a certain point in districts such as the Lunigiana, the Garfagnana or the Montagna Pistoiese, where there are plenty of small landowners and people still live on their farms or in tiny villages. Nor is it necessarily the case in Chianti or the Valdelsa, where the population is spread here and there, and the landscape has remained intensely "humanized", even though in many places we are dealing with a population of newcomers from the big cities of Tuscany, or even from other regions, and indeed from abroad (England, Germany, the United States). And at this point it is a question of the "weekend" or "holiday" house, of farming as a hobby, and producing wine and oil for family consumption or for the small-scale marketing of a very high-quality product.

What we have so far briefly outlined are those characteristics of the Tuscans which may be assessed from a quantitative point of view; nor can we afford in these pages to ignore these, and in fact should bear them in mind the whole time. But we have mentioned them chiefly to serve as a background to another, perhaps more important, question, and one less open to quantitative analysis. Who are the Tuscans? Do they really exist? If so, what relation do they bear to their "forefathers" (or, to put it slightly less rhetorically, the people who lived in the region before them?). These are the very "forefathers" who left such a copious and complex historical legacy that we moderns sometimes have no right to call it ours, and very often feel — and are called — unworthy of it.

All too much has been said about the "native character" of the Tuscans. For example, from the 13th century on we have been told about a so-called Tuscan School of Poetry, which in point of fact was anything but a "unified" school of poetry or of thought, and included poets from Arezzo, Pisa, Lucca and Florence, none of whom worried their heads about "unity" of language, subject, or culture in general — and how could it have been otherwise? Or if there was some measure of unity, it had nothing to do with the common denominator of "Tuscan" to which we moderns are apt to give too much *a posteriori* importance. It is true that Curzio Malaparte in his novels managed to create the "type" of the "damned Tuscan," but his creation had the shortcomings of every other such "type." It does not apply to any one case in particular, and having been brought to life by words it dies with them.

It would therefore be ridiculous to say that the Tuscans have an ethnical, historical and cultural identity which distinguishes them from their neighbours and sets its stamp on them over the course of centuries. This would be to ignore the falsity of borders and distinctions in the actual being and becoming of things in this world, and the illusoriness of making neat outlines and compact blotches of colour (as on a political map) out of what is in reality

part of a continuous process and a series of nuances.

A good example of all this is the dialect of the region — or rather, the "non-dialect." In a strict sense, there may possibly be a particular way of speaking, or more exactly a whole constellation of ways of speech. In short — and it is already a good deal — there is a "type of idiom" that we may call Tuscan.

As we all know, from the 13th century onward there was a "language problem" in Italy. In the course of a slow evolution over as much as six centuries, Tuscan — or rather, "educated Florentine" — asserted itself as the literary and "cultured" language throughout the nation, overcoming some fierce resistance and pretty weighty alternatives. This affirmation was based chiefly on the choice made by an élite in the context of a cultural development that ran parallel to the unifying political movement of the Risorgimento. Tuscan speech, or rather, educated Florentine, which Manzoni called "washing rinsed in the Arno," had a deep-rooted logic to recommend it, but it was by no means a necessary and compulsory solution. Indeed, it was a very deliberate choice, and one which (through state education) became actually imposed on the nation. And this should be said as regards relations between Tuscans and non-Tuscans: that even within the Tuscan region the choice of Florentine was the result of a slow but constant historical movement, for from the 13th century on Florence gradually gained the political ascendency in Tuscany. This ascendency met with some strong resistance, with some very worthy and reasonable alternatives, so that even at the end of the last century there were ringing challenges on the linguistic and literary plane. We need only mention Pietro Fanfani, a philologist from Collesalvetti, and his Vocabolario (1875), in which the "purist" definition is surrounded by a whole series of inducements aimed at safeguarding the non-Florentine "variants" of words and constructions.

However, the Tuscan "idiom," in its many variations which are

21. Andrea di Bonaiuto: The Church Militant and Triumphant, detail. Florence, Santa Maria Novella. Among the figures portrayed are Cimabue, Petrarch and Boccaccio.

22

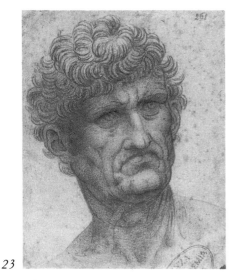

23

22. *Michelangelo: Head of a Woman. Florence, Collection of Prints and Drawings, Uffizi.*

23. *Leonardo da Vinci: Study of a Man. Venice, Academy.*

the object of much reciprocal bickering, is pretty clearly distinct from the Gallo-Italic dialects bordering on it to the north and east, both in vocabulary and in pronunciation; to such an extent that in certain districts in the Appennines (in spite of continual dealings to and fro) the watershed of dialect is no less evident, clear-cut and drastic than that of geography. The special characteristics of Tuscan speech are less clear in comparison with dialects to the south. Between many areas of south-eastern Tuscany and the bordering districts of Umbria and Lazio there are many affinities, and of ancient date, therefore not to be explained away by exchanges which have taken place in recent years; indeed, there were even more of them in the past. Plural endings in *—ora*, for example, have now disappeared from Tuscan speech in all its many variations, whereas before the 16th century they were common enough: Someone like Franco Sacchetti could perfectly naturally use the word *"luogora"* instead of *"luoghi."* In old Sienese the sounds *—nd—* and *—mb—* often became *—nn—* and *—mm—*, which is typical of Umbrian dialect, and then in the course of time dispensed with these assimilations, which in the 14th century were perfectly usual. The Arezzo district of the Valdichiana has been open to many influences, even to dialects as far afield as Emilia. But the speech of Arezzo and Siena still retains some traces of Umbria and the Marche, such as the verb *vendare* instead of *vendere*.

In any case, the last thing we should do in dealing with Tuscan speech is to generalize. Tuscans other than Florentines, for example, are highly incensed when accused of using words or pronunciations typical of Florence. To mention one instance, it is by no means the case that throughout the region the diphthong *—uo—* becomes simply *—o—* (as in the word *"uomo-omo"*), and still less that weak intervocal *—k—* and *—t—* sounds are always aspirated to *—h—*, according to a well-known phenomenon which has even been assigned an origin in Etruscan times.

On the other hand, in all its many variations, the Tuscan speech does possess a certain cohesiveness, and is fairly widespread as well, since we should remember that even Corsican belongs to the west-Tuscan group of dialects.

If it is difficult to speak of the "idiom" without generalizations and rhetoric, it is even harder to talk of the "traditions," expecially today, when the word is abused and exploited and so-called authentic folk and peasant traditions seem to sprout from every crevice. Connected for the most part with feast-days and fairs, they are good fun in themselves but very dubious from a historical point of view.

Let us begin by resisting the temptation to use labels that appear on the surface to be applicable, but in fact explain nothing. That is, we must avoid the pretence that everything is perfectly clear and in its place, as long as we can scatter around a few labels such as "alternative culturc" or "submerged culture." The point is, what do we know about our ancestors? What legacies have come down to us from them? Are we today really able to recognize an authentic tradition passed on from generation to generation, and to distinguish this from things brought back by revivals?

A number of students of southern Italy have described the culture of the "Mezzogiorno" as a "peasant culture" — a gross generalization immediately contradicted by others. But Tuscan culture, luckily, is so varied as to discourage any attempt of this kind. All the same, to define it as a "city culture" makes sense. We do not of course mean that Tuscany is a territory composed entirely of cities. We only wish to point out that ever since Etruscan times the country districts, the pasturelands, even the marshes and mountains of the region, have gravitated towards an urban centre, towards a governing class of landowners and producer-consumers living in urban settlements, and towards sacred places (temples in early times, cathedrals later) connected with the urban world. The refined way of life and the opulence of the manufactured products which we come across in Etruscan tombs is a result of this humanized and urbanized world. Even the Longobards, in spite of their nomadic and warlike past, adapted themselves to this mode of life. Without an appreciation of this "city-culture," in fact, we cannot understand the real character of the larger part of our landscape. Exception should be made, of course, for particular areas such as the Garfagnana, the Volterrano (area of Volterra), the Maremma, and the highest regions of the Appennines.

The legacy of language and dialect, archaeological discoveries, the layout of the territory, traditional tools and implements for both peasants and artisans, local festivals and saints' days: all these tend to divide Tuscany into areas analogous to those which emerge on the strictly linguistic level. There is a western region (around Lucca, Pisa and Livorno) which has certain characteristics in common with Liguria to the north and Emilia to the north-east; a central zone more or less contained in the triangle Florence, Siena-Volterra; an eastern area between the Arno and the Tiber and between Arezzo and Chiusi; and finally a southern area which includes the south of the province of Siena, Monte Amiata and the Maremma. For some years now the material evidence of these cultures has been collected in museums devoted to peasant culture and folk traditions, while (after a long stagnant period during which there was little or no interest in the tokens of past piety, and — especially after Vatican Council II – even indifference or scarcely-concealed intolerance) the dioceses and sanctuaries now frequently see to the preservation and cataloguing of relics, *ex-votos* and liturgical and devotional remains in their possession, even creating facilities for study. Much has also been done to collect and classify the oral culture of the region: stories, proverbs, songs, characteristic theatrical performances such as *"contrasti"* or *"bruscelli,"* ballads, ritualistic parodies such as *"Sega-la-vecchia,"* types of urban folk-drama connected with the *Commedia dell'arte*, and therefore with masques, rites and customs which may be traced back to a mythical and ritual substratum based on magic. All these have become the object of careful anthropological research.

The results of this quite rightly put paid to the commonplace according to which Tuscany, so rich in the monuments of a "great" cultural heritage, is on the other hand poor in respect to folk

24

25

24. *School of Leonardo da Vinci: Head of a Man. Florence, Collection of Prints and Drawings, Uffizi.*

25. *Leonardo da Vinci: Young Bacchus. Venice, Academy.*

26

26. A knight in Renaissance costume taking part in the Gioco del Ponte in Pisa.

culture, and in any case little concerned to preserve what it has. This is a legend which in the past was lent the weight of legality by parties with an axe to grind, who thought of it as a healthy march towards progress, though today it is mentioned only as an accusation.

All that was a pretext, and still is, whatever the reasons for it. If anything, the fact is that folk-culture is by its very nature anchored firmly to the places and the rhythms of life, to whatever is characteristic of daily living, to the systems of production and the division of labour. A culture composed of actions, of the skilful use of certain implements, of respect for the seasons with regard to work in the fields and the phases of the liturgical year, of customs linked to agriculture and craftsmanship, of songs and stories passed around the fireside, could not help but wilt under the impact of urbanization, industrialization, and the mass-media which have convulsed life and customs not only on a social level, but also on the plane of personal relations and the family. In these circumstances the recovery of certain traditions (especially those connected with festivals) sometimes comes close to being an archaeological experiment, and at others a rather demagogical piece of mystification, or purely recreational. There are a great number of anthropologists who maintain that when a tradition is dying because it no longer has the material conditions that sustained it, there is nothing to do but let it die, except possibly to give it a place on a few shelves in a museum, or in the pages of some learned volume.

On the other hand, there are the people themselves; for, over the last few years, often in a muddled, rough-and-ready way, people have tried to re-establish contact with the past. All over the region such things as periodical markets, fairs in town and country alike and the celebration of local saints' days have been expanded in cases where they had survived and revived where they had fallen into disuse. Festivals and feast-days are celebrated once again as such, and not reduced to something purely recreational; and in the meantime the "health industry" is rediscovering the "natural" and "genuine" food of days of yore, and telling us how to prepare it. Our fashionable modern-day troubadours and cabaret artists rework our old ballads and (albeit at the piano-bar level) come up with new versions of our songs of sweat and toil and hardship, but also (let it be said) of love and joy. Agreed that this is an ambiguous phenomenon, and one not without an eye to the consumer market, rather on the level of the renovation of the old farmhouses by the scions of the prosperous, city-dwelling bourgeoisie. But this is also a way of saving what is left of a legacy that otherwise would be fated to disappear, or to survive only as an archaeological find. And it is also a way of keeping memories alive, of feeling that one is living in that flow of things without which there is neither a sense of history nor an awareness of communal identity.

DOING, WORKING, PRODUCING

How well does one live in Tuscany? What the statistics say is "pretty well." It is true that there is a housing problem, but on the other hand there is no lack of weekend-houses in the countryside and the small villages, made available by the exodus towards the larger towns. Nor do our industrial suburbs have any "new towns" or the like, since there has been no large-scale immigration. Running water and central heating are now common features, and we are above the national average (and therefore on a par with the north-western regions, which are the most highly developed) in terms of ownership of cars and television sets. On the other hand, according to the statistics (and this may seem strange), the Tuscans do not spend a lot of money on performances on a cultural level. This may be partly due to their proverbial stinginess (which does not hold good for the Sienese, who have a reputation for extravagance), and partly because they are up to their necks in culture at home, and are fairly convinced that they actually invented it. Behind the statistics we have the "standard of living," as they say; but in any case the statistics give us quantitative figures, and these are of little use in assessing quality.

As regards net product and income per head, Tuscany is between sixth and eighth among the regions of Italy, after the northern regions. Out of about 1,400,000 employed persons, one can say that in round figures 500,000 work in industry, 130,000 (less than 10% of the total) in agriculture, and the rest in various trades. There are also about 100,000 unemployed and a certain number of people either under-employed or working at home, perhaps illegally. What we have therefore, over and above the facts and figures, is a pretty dynamic picture with a number of disquieting elements. Until the end of the 1950s Tuscany was still a prevalently agricultural region. With the economic boom of the early 1960s a process of industrial development began, and in certain areas such as that of Prato and the middle and lower Valdarno quickly reached a considerable level of intensity. However, to a large extent this retained what appears to be the typical and "original" characteristic of the region, which is the tendency towards small but dynamic firms. This brought with it a certain measure of economic weakness, but at the same time provided a fair degree of elasticity that made it substantially possible to face the crisis of the 1970s.

It seems that in Tuscany there is a leaning towards the small-scale, independent business. If we put this together with the old share-cropping method of farming, the result is certainly not favourable to the demands of modern agriculture. Also unfavourable to this is the very physical structure of the region, full as it is of hills and mountains. A considerable amount of the potentially productive land in Tuscany is in fact occupied by woods and rough pastures. In the remaining areas there is still a tendency towards what until a few years ago was the norm, which

27

28

27. *Hanks of wool set out to dry. Reggello (Florence).*

28. *Timber transport on Monte Amiata.*

29

30

29. Corn harvest near Monterchi (Arezzo).

30. Cobs set out to dry.

is to say mixed farming in which vines, olives and wheat co-exist in the same field. Now, however, grain has declined in favour of vines and olives, and the hilly areas of Tuscany have been largely given over to the more profitable specialized production of "*D.O.C.*" wines and olive oil, much of it for export. The great freeze of the winter of 1985 has, of course, reduced oil production to virtually nothing, forcing farmers to cut down or drastically prune almost all their trees; but on the other hand it is true that olives cultivated in the traditional manner gave a low yield, so that it has been often suggested that we should make use of the disaster of the freeze-up by rationalizing our techniques of production. Wines are, of course, very much at home in the area, especially in the celebrated Chianti district (which is, however, rather seriously threatened with destruction by quarries and cement-factories). But other areas producing fine wines are the Colli Senesi (Sienese Hills), the Sieve valley, the valley between Florence and Pistoia (Carmignano wines), and the island of Elba. Vegetable and fruit production does not exceed the requirements of the region, though some produce is of notably fine quality.

The woods are one of the glories of Tuscany, and also one of its problems. Its inhabitants do not always believe it, but Tuscany is one of the regions of Italy most abounding in forests, woodlands and wilderness, to a total of 870,000 hectares. From the economic point of view the woods are a great asset. The state-owned forests of Vallombrosa, Campigna and Camaldoli yield fine products for woodwork; the pinewoods along the coast and in the Valdarno give pine-nuts and resin; the chestnut woods yield not only their fruit (once a popular food and now after a long eclipse coming back into demand again) but also substances extracted from the bark and used in the tanning of leather; the deciduous bushes are used for making charcoal, while to the south of the Cècina we find an abundance of cork-oaks. Enormous stretches of territory have been reforested in the past few decades, while parts of the region have been repopulated with certain species of animals. In spite of this, Tuscany will never again be the hunter's paradise that it once was. There is a certain amount of game throughout the region, including wild boar in the more densely wooded areas. But the hunting of game, like fishing, was once linked less to the woodlands than to the marshes, and these have all but vanished.

Stock-raising is also in inevitable and irreversible decline. There are far fewer flocks of sheep migrating between the Apuan Alps and Appennines on the one hand and the coast of the Maremma on the other. At one time the festival of St. Luke (October 18th), at Impruneta near Florence, was a celebration of the return of the shepherds to the lowland pastures, but now, though retaining something of nobility, it has passed into the realm of folklore. On the other hand, especially in the districts of Siena and Grosseto, Sardinian shepherds have come in to fill the gap left by peasants who have abandoned numerous farms. The most highly-prized product is "pecorino", a sheep-cheese that is mild when fresh but grows increasingly strong with age. The cattle population, both for meat and for work, is restricted, though the Tuscan genius for small-scale enterprise has in recent years made strides with the immensely prized "Chianina" breed of beef cattle. The real "Florentine" beefsteak comes from the Chianina, but other traditional Tuscan breeds are the robust, attractive Maremmana and the Pisan, which gives good milk. An increasingly popular breed today is the Bruno-Alpina, which is imported. The pig is an old friend of the rural family economy, and at one time it was practically the only source of meat either fresh or preserved. However, in the districts of Siena and Arezzo in particular we find pig-raising on a larger scale, and the production of high-quality hams, salamis, etc.

It is very easy, and indeed a current intellectual affectation, to speak ill of the "return to the soil" as a kind of chic mystification, of luxury tourism draped with health-manias. The cowboys who once gave such a hard lesson to Colonel "Buffalo Bill" Cody have in turn become a rarity, and their place has been taken by Sunday cowboys, those who patronize "agritourism" or like to ride out from the expensive hotels of Punta Ala. All this may be rather irritating. All the same, there has been a revival of the glorious tradition of horse-breeding in the Maremma, while the "new romanticism" of looking for tiny patches of nature still intact or reconstituted at vast expense has here and there (also in the Maremma) led to the reappearance of the buffalo. A consumer's garden of Eden? Even if it were so, our time has committed worse crimes. It is a pity, though, that no "agritourism" in the world thinks of saving the few poor donkeys, mules and hinnies. After giving valiant service for centuries, transporting people and things, these humble poor relations of the horse are now disappearing from the region: only a few thousand are left. Readers of Pinocchio will also lament the extinction of the little Tuscan ass with its tender, intelligent eyes (that donkeys are stupid is a calumny spread by schoolboys afraid of the competition). This little animal is no longer even to be found as an ingredient of mortadella, which in any case is an Emilian kind of salame, and no great favourite in Tuscany.

Since we have spoken about hunting and stock-raising, completeness demands that we should briefly mention fishing. And here there is really little to gladden our hearts. Even if fresh fish and crustaceans never seem to be lacking in the summer markets or at parties on the Argentario, the waters of the Tyrrhenian are stinting and subject to constant impoverishment. Gone are the days when there were tunny-fishing nets to be seen on Elba, though a small catch is still made in the Tuscan Archipelago. However, Viareggio, Livorno, the Argentario and Portoferraio are still fishing centres of a certain note, while the occasional lobster is caught at Montecristo and Giglio. The total production only amounts to a few hundred tons. The fishing-fleet of the big frozen-fish firm of Genepesca are commissioned in Livorno, but they sail down to Africa or even towards America.

On the other hand, if the woodlands, and hunting and fishing, are not as flourishing as they were, the reasons are well-known, and range from the growth of industry, to the overpopulation

31. Earthenware kiln in Impruneta (Florence).

32. Terracotta wares produced in Impruneta.

33

33. *In some areas of Tuscany nets are placed permanently around the trunks of the olive trees. When the olives are ripe, the nets are spread out to collect the ripe fruit. This olive grove is near Caprona (Pisa).*

during the summer months and the question of pollution. Nor are these neutral causes and inevitable happenings, but the results of choices taken deliberately, even if not always properly controlled. In these circumstances the development of industry, and above all manufacturing on the plane of craftsmanship has in the last few years reached considerable levels in terms of quantity, and by no means always at the expense of quality. In this field the local talent for free enterprise and for producing high-quality goods have gone hand in hand, with the result that products are on the average really good, and sometimes excellent.

The small firm, the break-up of larger units into smaller ones, and the accompanying subdivision of capital... When people seriously believed in a "one-way" economic development, these features were long considered the limits of the capacity of the business world in Tuscany, which has often been called narrow-minded, egoistic, pusillanimous and out of date. In the long run, however, it has been realized that these characteristics, which from some points of view do certainly hold things back, were in fact not so much a weakness as a strength to an economic world unwilling to abandon the level of individual craftsmanship and move onto an industrial scale; and this not always purely for reasons of economic profitability.

Another long-established feature of Tuscany, which we have mentioned in terms of culture and politics, is that it is "polycentric"; that is, with many centres rather than one. On the level of productivity and labour this leads to a system in which the availability of certain raw materials is in tune with many long-established methods (or even secrets) of manufacture, and pride in one's work, in the best sense of the word.

Such areas are sometimes known as "islands" of productivity, and the most conspicuous of them, with roots stretching far back into history, is the textile zone of Prato, where the old "ragshops" have long since been converted into highly modernized, active concerns. In second place come the tanneries and the shoemakers of the "leather district" which stretches between the lower Valdarno and the Valdinievole, along with the "furniture district" more or less in the triangle described by Cascina, Pontedera and Ponsacco, and its more recent rival in the zone between Prato and Pistoia. Most of this stuff is mass-produced, but there is a proportion of traditional, handmade wares.

Other districts well worthy of mention are those of the glass trade (between Empoli and Montelupo), of ceramics (at Sesto Fiorentino and between Montelupo and Signa), and paper-making, including some beautiful factories, some of ancient date, near Barga in the Serchio valley, around Pescia and at Colle Valdelsa, while ready-made clothes are produced in abundance in the Empoli area. Impruneta is the home of famous fired bricks and tiles, the very same that once roofed Brunelleschi's dome on the cathedral of Florence. Stia is a well-known centre for wrought-iron, while Scarperia is famed for its fine cutlery. Goldsmith's work is now concentrated chiefly in and around Arezzo, with mass-production accompanied by the highest

34

35

standards of craftsmanship. The working of various kinds of stone (alabaster at Volterra, marble around Carrara, *"pietra serena"* in the Fiesole hills, round Empoli and in the Alto Mugello) is dependent on the quarries existing in these areas. Florence, of course, is a kind of compendium of all these specialities, a shop-window for expert craftsmanship that in many cases reaches the level of art itself. We might mention the workshop ("Opificio") for semi-precious stones, the leather-working school at Santa Croce, and the goldsmiths' shops which are traditionally clustered on and around the Ponte Vecchio. But above all else it is in the world of high fashion that Florence is really and truly on a world level, with its shows and its fashion parades at Palazzo Pitti, as well as its boutiques which are often linked with those of the Great Names in Rome, Milan, Paris, London and New York.

In comparison to the many and famous enterprises thriving in the world of the arts and crafts, "industry" in Tuscany is in what we might call a minor key. In this case the small scale of the firms themselves and the capital involved might have slowed up the rate of development. But this might not be such a bad thing after all, considering those unique things that make Tuscany renowned throughout the world, such as the landscape, the specialized agricultural products (wine and oil in particular), along with tourism and the good standard of living in general. It may be that these would not altogether harmonize with intensive industrialization. All the same, we have a steel industry with its great blast furnaces at Piombino, foundries in Florence and around Livorno, the production of precision-instruments in Florence, and of motorcycles in Pontedera, while there are shipyards at Livorno and Viareggio, chemical plants at Rosignano and near Volterra, and cement-works in the province of Florence. This development has had an inevitable impact on the environment, and has brought about constant arguments on one side and the other. There are the old Progressives left over from the Thirties, for whom industrial development was the sure sign of a higher level of social and technological progress, cost what it may, and there are the

36

34. *Grape harvest.*

35. *Pressing grapes by foot: a practice that is now rare.*

36. *Mechanized division of grapes from the stalks, in Greve in Chianti.*

37

38

37. *Cattle raising in Valdichiana.*

38. *A textile factory in Prato (Florence).*

ecologists who dream of a region made into an enormous Park of natural and artistic beauties. Between these two parties a middle way is now being sought for, in order to preserve and administrate a legacy of incomparable beauty.

Where industry and the environment do still come to blows is in the field of mines and quarries. Tuscany was at one time volcanic, and still has its residue of thermal phenomena, but it is also a land of minerals and metals. Apart from the marble quarries of the Apuan Alps, home of Carrara Marble, we should mention the iron mined in Elba, mercury from Monte Amiata, endogenous steam and borax from Lardarello and lignite from the Upper Valdarno. Tuscany yields all the mercury and pyrite in Italy, and in these sectors is in fourth place in the world. But the Colline Metallifere yield not only pyrite but lead, and therefore — or until only a few years ago — silver as well. Massa Marittima is a positive capital of the mining industry, and mineralogy is part of its local history and culture.

What we have said about industry and craftsmanship already gives us the outlines of the main sources of Tuscan exports: handicrafts, olive oil, wine, vegetable products, plants and flowers (with nurseries at Pistoia and large-scale horticulture around Pescia), products of the metallurgic and mechanical industries, textiles, glass products, and finally the famous sweetmeats of Siena, such as "*panforte*" and "*ricciarelli.*"

All the same, one of the chief industries of Tuscany, and one of the most profitable, is still tourism. If the winter-sports centres in the Appennines (with Abetone in the vanguard) are at this time of only secondary importance, of greater interest are the many thermal springs, from the celebrated baths at Montecatini to the old-established ones in the provinces of Lucca, Pisa and Siena. The beaches are attractive and reasonably well-equipped all the way from Sarzana to Grosseto, but the majority of the summer crowds choose the Versilia and the coast between Cècina and Piombino, though there are also areas of luxury tourism at Punta Ala, on the Argentario and on the islands. The artistic legacy of places incomparably endowed with masterpieces (and we are not alluding only to big cities such as Florence, Pisa or Siena) bring tourists by the million from all corners of the earth. Naturally enough, not all tourists in Tuscany are foreigners (among the German, American and British visitors we have in recent years seen increasing numbers of Japanese). In point of fact nearly two-thirds of the tourists are Italians from other regions of the country, or even the Tuscans themselves. There is a large network of hotels (second only in terms of quantity to the regions of Emilia-Romagna and the Veneto), but it is well supported, in line with the Tuscan tradition, by small-scale enterprises, such as "pensions" (especially in Florence and on the coast), as well as camping-sites and hostels which serve to meet the most recent wave of tourism, composed of young people. The general picture would be fairly satisfactory if profiteering were not so rife in the property and building markets, combining with the horrors of pollution to undermine it.

39

40

41

It may at first sight appear odd that this region, so open to visitors from abroad, and therefore so accustomed to comparing itself with other cultures, is also known for the aggressiveness of its inhabitants, a feature that may sometimes have its charm, but also its inconveniences. Faced with a visitor, even if he be a tourist with good money in his pocket, your average Tuscan does not show a lot of enthusiasm. Someone who pays a visit of a few days or even weeks might easily slip by unnoticed, in a place accustomed for decades to seeing people just like him; but someone who decides to put down roots for a while sooner or later comes up against a wall built not so much of suspicion and discourtesy as of a mixture of circumspection and indifference.

And it may also seem strange that a region with so many great cultural traditions barely keeps above the national average in terms of education. In Tuscany there are three universities, at Florence, Pisa and Siena (with a branch in Arezzo), as well as a vast number of institutes of higher education, many branches of foreign (largely American) universities, as well as renowned institutions such as the Collegio di Poggio Imperiale in Florence and the Convitto Nazionale Cicognini in Prato, both of them by tradition boarding-schools for the upper classes, or at least the wealthy. In spite of this your average Tuscan does not seem to have too much faith in education and culture, and in this regard he is put at an advantage throughout the region by the "family firm", and therefore the possibility of finding work positively "at home". The result is that he tends to leave school early and take up a money-making job as soon as possible. As far as this is concerned, sociologists and historians of education never fail to point out that until the 15th century the average Tuscan was perfectly capable of filling in his own registers of produce etc., and indeed this is proved by contemporary documents. It was only later on that illiteracy became so widespread that when Italy was unified it was as high as 70% throughout the region. It would appear that between the 16th and 18th centuries there was a period of stagnation hard to overcome; and this in fact coincides with what

39. Blocks of marble in the quarry of Pian della Fioba (Massa) in the Apuan Alps.

40. Nineteenth-century ironworks at Ravi, in the Colline Metallifere.

41. An old cement factory in Calenzano (Florence).

42. *The Solvay chemical industry at Rosignano (Livorno).*

43. *The town of Larderello.*

44. *The steelworks at Piombino.*

we know of cultural tendencies throughout Italy, and indeed throughout Europe.

But the fact is that "culture" is not only a matter of literacy, let alone of faithful attendance at school. The streets of our towns and cities have for centuries been lined with works of art, both religious and civic, that have no match in the world, not only in terms of excellence but also of number. They in themselves were the schools of taste, and character, and aesthetics, for the Tuscans. It seems to me that a child in San Gimignano, who has left school at fifteen but has nonetheless grown up among the mediaeval towers of the town, and its marvellously frescoed church, in a position to meet tourists from all over the world, able to see the exhibitions organized by the Commune and the operas performed in the piazza during the summer, has had as good a schooling as an 18 year-old with 3 A-levels, as it were, from any town in Lombardy or Calabria, where there are less than no cultural resources and the landscape is desolate and destroyed. I contend that one learns more in a Florentine workshop on the left bank of the Arno than in any art school in Italy, where one scratches the surface of a few textbooks thrust upon one by the Ministry of Education, while Giotto, Botticelli and Leonardo da Vinci are cut down to a paragraph a head. And all this while they are not merely at hand, but staring you in the face every day of your life.

From all this, without wishing to generalize (needless to say), emerge the two "exports" most widespread in Tuscany, and the most typical of this land. In these pages written by a true-born Tuscan, the reader will already have discerned the first: this is an absolutely stubborn pride. The other is one of the foundations for this pride, an artistic and cultural legacy unique in the whole world, and this not only because it is incomparable in terms of beauty and of abundance, but also (and above all) because it is deep-rooted in the explicit, conscious memory of the people of Tuscany. By which I mean, of course, history. And it is to history that we now have to turn.

MEMORY AND IDENTITY
THE ETRUSCANS

Several tens of thousands of years ago the upper valley of the Arno was a huge lake surrounded by dense forests. Today it abounds in lignite and fossils. The bones discovered bear witness to the fact that around Montevarchi and down the Valdichiana was the haunt of elephant, rhinoceros, deer, bears, big cats and monkeys. In the Apuan Alps, Versilia, the Lunigiana and the Garfagnana there are numerous natural caves with traces of fires and artefacts that may date back to the Palaeolithic, Mesolithic or Neolithic ages. This covers a considerable span of time, between 2 million and 3 thousand years before Christ.

It was around the latter date that man began to work in metal here, as well as stone. In the Apuan Alps, dating from about that time, we find numerous metal objects (silver, lead and copper), in conjunction with new funeral rites which were evidently brought in by peoples who had recently arrived in the area. Throughout the whole of the Appennines there is much evidence of the Bronze Age and the Villanovian period. However it is between the 2nd and the 1st centuries B.C., corresponding to the beginning of the Iron Age, that the southern part of what is now Tuscany begins to emerge. This is in fact the area which over the centuries saw the growth of the great culture which was destined to characterize the whole territory and give it its first name.

It is perhaps between the 9th and 8th centuries B.C. that we may begin to speak of an Etruscan civilization and an Etruscan people, since at that time the territory between the Tyrrhenian Sea and the valleys of the Arno and the Tiber became densely settled by these people. With their funeral rites involving cremation, which we usually associate with Villanovian culture, they have by some scholars been connected with those peoples who gave rise to the culture of "urn burial" in Central Europe and Northern Italy towards the end of the Bronze Age. Various theories have been put forward about the origins of the Etruscans. On the authority of Herodotus (who mentioned Lydia as their original homeland) they have been said to have come from Asia Minor, or according to other theories from the north. Finally, on the basis of hints furnished by Dionysius of Halicarnassus, they have been held to have been "aboriginal": that is, that they were related to peoples inhabiting Italy before the arrival of the Indo-Europeans. However, the historical and archaeological data in our possession make it unlikely that the Etruscan "nation" came into being as the result of some sudden event — such as an invasion by a "new" people — or indeed over a relatively short span of years. On the contrary, it is now commonly held that it came about slowly, with the gradual formation of those ethnical and cultural features which we are accustomed to think of as genuinely Etruscan.

Much has been said about the Etruscan "mystery," mostly concerning the mythical and religious features of that ancient people, with their strong tendency towards the techniques of

45

45. Objects found in a Villanovian tomb. Florence, Archeological Museum.

46. Etruscan earrings. Volterra, Guarnacci Museum.

47. The entrance of the Etruscan tomb of Montagnola at Quinto (Florence).

divination and deep-seated burial rites. It is to these that we owe the vast majority of our knowledge of the mental world and everyday life of the Etruscans. The same is true of the language, the basic structures of which are still hard to understand today, even if we do succeed in reading it letter by letter and grasping the sense (we have, however, come this far by way of a Greek alphabet taught to the Etruscans by emigrants from Euboea during the 8th century B.C.). Judging from analogies with the known language of Lemnos in the 6th century B.C., it has been suggested that Etruscan (like the language of Lemnos) is a relic of a language spoken throughout the Mediterranean before the arrival of the Indo-Europeans. In any case, from the 3rd to the 1st centuries B.C., the Romans overwhelmed and decimated the Etruscans, who gave up speaking their own language entirely, particularly after 90 B.C., the year in which Etruria was granted Roman citizenship.

The great flourishing of Etruscan civilization was therefore between the 8th and the 4th centuries B.C., and it is significant that this coincides with the considerable population growth which took place in the 9th and 8th centuries, and also with the arrival of the first Greek colonists. The latter, settling in Campania, showed a great deal of interest in the metal resources of the island of Elba, and of the whole area between the coast and the Tiber. The exploitation of the mineral resources and intense activity in trade and handicrafts created a flourishing economy and a taste for luxury among the ruling classes in the towns, whose solid well-being is attested by the wealth of precious and refined objects with which they were buried. We are told by Greek historians that in the 7th and 6th centuries there was a thorough-going "thalassocracy" of the Tyrrhenian, during which Etruscan civilization — profoundly influenced by Greek culture — extended south of the Tiber as far as Campania and north of the Appennines into the Po valley, where such centres emerged as Félsina (Bologna) and Spina (at the mouth of the river). That was the period of the so-called "dodecapolis" (the "twelve cities," although in fact they were more than twelve). This was a federation of city-states that were completely independent, but at the same time strongly linked by the awareness of their common ethnic and cultural roots, expressed above all in language and religion. The wealthiest and most important of these were at first the coastal towns such as Populonia, Vetulonia, Roselle, Talamone, Cosa (now Ansedonia), Vulci, Tarquinia, Pyrgi (now Santa Severa) and Caere (now Cerveteri). But the towns of the interior soon gained in importance, with the rise of Fiesole, Volterra, Arezzo, Cortona, Perugia, Chiusi, Volsinii, Falerii and Veii. Trade and communications were assured by a network of roads, running both parallel to the coast (to connect the coastal centres) and at right angles to it to link up the inland towns. Even in those days Tuscany could qualify as a "land of cities," some of which were more ancient than Rome. And even in those days there was the tendency towards the particular, the local, the specific — a tendency that has remained as a "genuine feature" of the history and art of the region. For every centre, even in those times, had its particular way of making objects, building and decorating tombs and necropolises, or shaping and colouring pottery.

THE ROMAN RESHUFFLE

It was in the 6th century that an Etruscan dynasty, the Tarquins, became kings of Rome, while in the same century the Etruscans, allied to the Carthaginians, were apparently successful in repelling the expansionistic aims of the Greek colonists and keeping a firm grip on the Tyrrhenian. Nevertheless, by the end of that century Etruscan power was shaken by events such as the abortive conquest of Cumae in 525 B.C., the fall of the house of Tarquin in Rome and the rebellion of Latium in 510-505, the growing aggressiveness of the Appennine peoples (Umbrians, Sabines, Samnites), the defeat off Cumae of the Etruscan fleet by that of Siracuse (474 B.C.) and the sack of Caere in 384, once again by Siracuse. By the early 4th century, shaken also by a wave of invasion by the Celts (who got as far as Rome), the power of the Etruscans was prostrate. After that the Etruscans were in no position to resist the advance of Rome, which overran the independent cities one by one, or forced them into disadvantageous alliances, while at the same time founding new centres and gaining control of the network of communications.

The Roman conquest was not confined to destroying the bases of Etruscan civilization, even where formally and in appearance these were left intact. On the contrary, it brought about a thorough reshuffle of the territory and social structure of Tuscany, favouring the appropriation of the *ager publicus* by the patrician families of the new capital, distributing lands near the old cities to veterans of the Roman army, and finally taking over the road network and rearranging it to make "all roads lead to Rome." In Etruscan times the roads were laid out in such a way as to facilitate communications between the coast and the interior, and the Romans modified all this to provide easy passage to and from the capital. The roads hence came to run prevalently north-south, leading to the decline of the towns which were "out of line." The Via Clodia, the Via Cassia, and above all the Via Aurelia between Rome and Pisa, became the chief axes of the new system.

This automatically brought about the economic and cultural decay of many Etruscan centres, a tendency which Augustus attempted to contain by making Etruria part of the *VII Regio* and giving birth to a programme of colonization and social and economic reorganization. These measures included the establishment of huge *villae* farmed by slaves and of manufactures in many of the towns. But the process of decay could not be stopped, and in the 2nd century had already taken on several chronic features: the towns began to drop in population, while the southerly coastal areas began gradually to turn into marshes, a process that in every sense changed the *Maritima* into the

48

49

48. *The ruins of a Roman villa at Porto Santo Stefano.*

49. *Ruins of the Roman floor mosaic at Vulci.*

50

50. *Mino da Fiesole: Tomb of the Marquis Ugo of Tuscany. Florence, Badia Fiorentina.*

Maremma. In the early 5th century A.D. the description of the coast of Etruria in the *De Reditu Suo* of Rutilius Claudius Namatianus gives us a picture of decay and pitiful desolation. In the 6th century the wars between the Greeks and the Goths and (from 570 on) the arrival of the Longobards and the slaughter and destruction that accompanied their earliest settlements seemed to deliver the coup de grâce to a region shattered by outbreaks of smallpox and the plague, and sorely tried during the same period by natural disasters such as ruinous floods.

FROM THE LONGOBARDS TO FEUDALISM

The Longobards organized the region into a duchy with its main centre at Lucca, although it stood in the middle of a flood plain. During the two centuries of their dominion the road-network deteriorated still further. The Via Aurelia became almost impassable, being exposed to erosion by the sea and the spread of the marshes; and also marshy was the Via Cassia, which ran from Pistoia and Florence to Rome by way of Chiusi and Bolsena. In the section through the Val di Chiana it was also liable to attacks by the Byzantines coming from the Adriatic coast, where the Exarch had his seat. All through the 10th century Tuscany was a land of fevers, of ruined monuments, of settlements abandoned or sparsely populated because of the drop in population and the tendency of the inhabitants to live in out-of-the-way places for reasons of safety. The historical and archaeological documents of the time all agree in giving us the picture of a life of hardship, with agriculture at a subsistence level, the plains half abandoned, large stretches of once-cultivated land reduced to grassland, marshes or woods, while the dwellings were wretched huts or — especially in the south of the area — caves.

The marshes that swamped the coast-road and the dangers of the eastern route had even in Longobard times made it necessary to have a new road to Rome through the centre of the region. This indeed came about with the increasing importance of the *Mons Bardonis* road (the Cisa Pass) and consequently of the road leading from there to Rome by way of Lucca, the mid-Valdarno, the Val d'Elsa, Siena, Radicofani, Acquapendente, Bolsena, Viterbo and Sutri.

The Longobard rearrangement of Tuscan territory disrupted and cancelled out the order set up in the region at the end of the Roman Empire. Diocletian had in fact united what came more and more to be known as *Tuscia* to Umbria, while in 370 Tuscia had been divided into the *suburbicaria* to the south of the Arno and the *annonaria* to the north; as governor of the whole region there was a *Corrector*, with his seat in Florence. But the function of Florence as the chief centre did not survive the Longobard invasion, nor did the city succeed in reclaiming importance after the year 774, when the territory became a "march" of the Carolingian world. In fact Florence lay off the route of the new road which came down from the Cisa Pass and (due to the fact that it was chiefly the artery used by pilgrims travelling from France to Rome) was already known as the Via Francigena. The Tuscan metropolis of the late Middle Ages therefore remained Lucca, which in the course of the 11th century was joined by Pisa.

A certain amount of sea-going and trade had survived in Pisa even under the Longobards, but throughout the late Middle Ages it was an exception on a coast that was seriously depressed not only because of the encroaching marshes, but also due to the Saracen and Norman incursions which from the 8th to the 10th centuries were the scourge of the Tuscan shores no less than those of Corsica and Sardinia. This caused, or hastened, the decline of once-flourishing urban centres, along with the related phenomenon of the transfer of the sees of the bishops towards nearby towns further inland: the see of Luni moved to Sarzana, that of Populonia to Massa Marittima, that of Roselle to Grosseto.

During the 10th century, however, we begin to discern a few signs of reawakening due to the efforts of the marquises of Tuscany, both at the end of that century with the famous Marquis Ugo, and at the beginning of the next century, when the marquisate passed to the powerful family of the Counts of Canossa, who between feudal titles and alodial estates possessed a real and proper "empire" that stretched from the Tuscan-Emilian Appennines as far as Modena, Reggio, Mantua and Ferrara. Their power, however, began to wane after the death in 1115 of the "great" Countess Matilde, who with Gregory VII and the emperor Henry IV had been a protagonist of the period known as the Wars of the Investitures. In exchange, 12th-century Tuscany was divided up between the great feudal families such as the Malaspina who controlled the Lunigiana, the Alberti with their vast feuds between the Appennines and the mid-Valdarno, the Guidi who dominated the Casentino, and the Aldobrandeschi who were powerful in Siena. Beside these noble dynasties were lesser feudal families who played a minor but often far from negligible role. Many of them settled in the cities, which were even then beginning the process of recovery, thereby creating a town-dwelling aristocracy that was a feature of the first phase of the movement of the Communes, or the free city-states.

51

52

51. *Niccolò Gerini: Two Bankers. Prato, San Francesco.*

52. *The florin, Florence's gold coin.*

THE AGE OF THE COMMUNES

The characteristic feature of the 11th and 12th centuries in Tuscany was in fact the revival of trade, manufacturing, and the civil and economic life of the cities. While Lucca, in the absence of the powers of the marquisate, went into a slow but dignified decline, Pisa succeeded in linking its rise to power with the struggles (first in alliance but later in competition with Genoa) to free the Tyrrhenian from the menace of the Saracen pirates and gain control of Corsica and Sardinia. In the second half of the 11th century a bitter religious and political struggle broke out in

53

53. *Luca della Robbia: The emblem of the Wool Guild (Arte della Lana). Florence, Orsanmichele.*

Pisa, Lucca and Florence, connected with the reforms of the Church at that time. In a Tuscany until then accustomed to the presence of great monasteries that were also feudal overlords, such as the abbey of San Salvatore on Monte Amiata, these events led to the foundation of new and typically Tuscan religious orders, such as the Vallombrosians and the Camaldolensians, who even built abbeys in the cities, making a considerable contribution to their political lives.

Pisan dominance was sanctioned and confirmed by the movement of the Crusades. Even though late in the day, the city took part in the First Crusade, and in 1100, though only for a short time, its archbishop became the Latin Patriarch of Jerusalem; but it also had an important role in the Second and Third Crusades. These exploits gained Pisa a leading place in the Mediterranean mercantile world of the time, and the city founded trading colonies not only on the coasts of Syria and Palestine but also at Byzantium and in Africa. Towards the end of the 12th century, we begin to discern the emergence of those elements which caused Pisa to lose the leading role in the area. Her constant loyalty to the emperors of the Swabian house, whose political designs were largely shattered by the resistance of the popes, and the rise of the vigorous communal movement, did nothing to help Pisa. Nor did she show herself capable of coping at one and the same time with the pressure exerted by her two great rivals, Genoa on the sea and Florence, which was pressing from the hinterland.

At first sight it might appear that the characteristic feature of Tuscany during the 12th and 13th centuries (not very different from what happened in most of central and northern Italy at that time) was the struggle between the Guelphs (supporters of papal power) and the Ghibellines, who backed the power of the Holy Roman Empire in the fight between two "universal" authorities. But this had little to do with great political or ethical principles, and was really the excuse for contesting frontiers, dominating the routes of communication, and seizing new markets close at hand or otherwise. The "chessboard" structure of it, according to which if one city is Ghibelline the others around it become Guelph, and vice versa, is clear proof that these choices were nothing but pretexts. The same thing is reflected in the struggles between the aristocratic families of each single town, so that where the Guelphs were on top the families opposing those in power immediately declared themselves Ghibellines, and so on. But the reality is not to be found on the political face of things, but on the contrary in a really savage struggle for power, which saw cities pitted against feudal overlords, or one town against another, or even family against family in one and the same place.

An objective cause of political instability throughout the 12th century was the great number of free Communes that set themselves up in the region. This phenomenon was accompanied by the tendency of the larger ones to domineer over the smaller, or at least to make them into allies, needless to say on unequal terms. In other words the communal "city-state" tended by its very nature to grow larger and to transform itself into a territorial state.

This was necessary to establish and maintain free circulation on the roads and to control the markets. Thus, with occasional variants, there came about a difficult equilibrium which, however, implied a constant clash between a Guelph alliance (Florence and Lucca together with cities outside Tuscany, such as Genoa and Perugia) and a Ghibelline league (Pisa, Siena, Pistoia, Arezzo). Also during the 13th century the quarrels between the old aristocratic families who formed the governing classes of the old Communes, with their knightly rank and way of life, and houses and towers in the towns and lands outside it, were added to by the struggle (political, but also in part social) of the non-aristocratic citizens who possessed new forms of economic power. These were the bankers, merchants and manufacturers (above all of textiles) who had liquid cash with which to challenge the power of the old nobility and take a hand in the government. This was the battle between the magnates and the populace, in which "populace" must be understood to mean the classes of businessmen, producers, shopkeepers and so on, all organized into professional associations known as "*Arti*" (Guilds) or Corporations. Towards the end of the 13th century this led in more or less all the cities of Tuscany to the formation of governments dominated by the big business organizations. Once they had come to power these organizations became strongly conservative. The bankers and manufacturers (especially in textiles) who were also the protagonists and leaders in the political field tended to marry into the old aristocracy and to inherit its mental attitudes and ways of life, and they invested a conspicuous part of their business profits in buying land.

On the other hand they did not intend to lose a dominance that they had fought so hard to gain. To this end they had to protect themselves against the rise of the lower classes, socially subordinate to them, by attempting to regulate or even prevent any possible political role for the masses. These, for their part, aimed to get a say in the government. Beside the "*Popolo grasso*" (the "Fat populace" whom we could very roughly compare with the upper middle class) there emerged in the 14th century a "*Popolo magro*" or "Lean populace" composed of small businessmen and artisans, also provided with their corporations, and even the crowd of employees and subordinates ("*Popolo minuto*") who were forbidden to enter public affairs and refused the right to set up organizations. In the second half of the 14th century, when as well as a general drop in population culminating in the Black Death of 1348 there was a grave social and economic depression throughout the whole of Europe, the lower classes made their voice heard in a number of uprisings, such as the famous revolt of the *Ciompi* (employees of the Wool Guild) in Florence in 1378. These were immediately suppressed by the governments, the reins of which were in the hands of the big businessmen.

54

55

54. Illumination from the Biadaiolo manuscript: Distribution of wheat. Florence, Laurentian Library.

55. Chigi manuscript: Factional strife in Florence. Vatican, Apostolic Library.

Tuscan Festas

Quite a number of towns in Tuscany have their own special way of celebrating Carnival, the most famous of all being Viareggio with its parade of allegorical floats. But Carnival is only one of a number of feast-days that are not peculiar to Tuscany. There are numberless fairs, and festas and whatnot. For the most part, perhaps, they are the result of rather dubious "revivals," and fishing up old traditions to make money out of them, in the same way that "local customs" and "country taverns" have sprouted up like mushrooms.

Nevertheless, a lot of good things remain. For example, in the middle of October you simply have to go to Impruneta for the Fair of San Luca, which at one time coincided with the date at which the flocks of sheep, on their way down to winter in the Maremma, were assembled here at the famous shrine of the Virgin Mary. The "Rificolona," in which people parade through the streets of Florence with Chinese lanterns to celebrate the feast marking the birth of the Virgin (September 8th), has deep roots in the consciousness of the people and sound historical origins. Indeed it appears that it is derived from the "fierucolone," or processions of the women from the surrounding countryside coming in to Florence on the eve of the festival in good time to sell their wares next day in the Piazza della Santissima Annunziata. In Pisa the display of lights of San Ranieri is worth seeing, while in Florence it is rather sad to see the great religious and civic festival of San Giovanni celebrated only with fireworks.

However, if you have a chance, there are several other festas worth the trip. At Querceta near Forte dei Marmi, on the second Sunday after Easter, there is the donkey "palio" (i.e. donkey race), at Pienza there is the cheese fair on the first Sunday in September. But above all there are the "butterate" in the Maremma. These are Tuscan "rodeos" in which cowboys and their mounts compete in agility and ability. It is well known around here that the cowboys of the Maremma were challenged by the world-famous troupe of that over-inflated gasbag Buffalo Bill, and that they beat the Americans hands down.

LE RIFICOLONE.

I

II

III

I. *The festa of the Rificolone in Piazza Santissima Annunziata in Florence. Florence, Museo di Firenze Com'era.*

II. *An engraving showing the Gioco del Ponte in Pisa. Florence, Uffizi, Collection of Prints and Drawings.*

III. *An allegorical float at the Viareggio Carnival.*

IV-V. *The Giostra del Saracino at Arezzo.*

VI-VII-VIII. *The Calcio in Costume in Florence.*

56

57

56. *Domenico Ghirlandaio: Birth of the Virgin, detail of ladies in 15th-century clothes. Florence, Santa Maria Novella.*

57. *Jacopo Pontormo: Portrait of Cosimo the Elder. Florence, Uffizi.*

THE RISE OF FLORENCE

In any case, in spite of numerous crises and periods of marking time, it was the city of Florence, with its ruling class of bankers and producers of woollen textiles, which imposed its dominion on the whole of Tuscany. In 1252 the Florentines were among the first to mint a gold coin of their own, the florin, which along with the Venetian ducat very soon became the currency par excellence of the entire European side of the Mediterranean, and was in effect the main basis for pursuing a "power policy." Pisa, exhausted by its constant struggles with Genoa, and crippled by the end of the Crusades which had put its colonial system into a state of crisis, ceased to be a real rival at the end of the 13th century. Siena had in the 13th century established an important banking system, but it could not keep pace with Florence, which apart from all else enjoyed the support of the two great religious and political powers of the early 14th century, the papacy and the French monarchy. In spite of this, for much of the 14th century it still seemed anyone's bet in Tuscany. For example, Castruccio Castracani, an audacious Ghibelline chief with a good head for politics, succeeded in becoming lord of Pistoia and Lucca, and making them the centres of a territory that posed a great threat to Florence. Later on, at the end of the century, a similar threat appeared to be posed by a non-Tuscan ruler, Giangaleazzo Visconti, Duke of Milan. He had a great number of supporters in Tuscany, who saw him (if nothing else) as the only hope of preventing the dominance of Florence. And in fact as we see from the letters of the city's Humanist chancellor, Coluccio Salutati, a tireless opponent of Visconti, Florence lost no opportunity of presenting herself (and not just to Tuscans, but to the whole of Central Italy) as the most reliable defender of "freedom" against the "tyrants." These "tyrants" were the party leaders or knights of feudal origin who as early as the end of the 13th century had seized power in many towns in Lombardy, the Veneto and Emilia, making themselves "Lords" of them on the pretext that these towns were unable to sort out their political squabbles and institutional crises. What is called "*signoria*" (overlordship) is in fact not a Tuscan phenomenon, even if there is no lack of instances of it all through the region (from Arezzo to Lucca, from Cortona to Pisa and Siena). And most of all it is not a Florentine phenomenon, since in Florence the various families fighting each other for power never managed to find a successful leader until the middle of the 15th century. In the late 14th century, and well into the 15th, Florence was therefore governed by an oligarchy of wealthy families. To the economic power which they derived from banking, wool manufacturing or other highly remunerative activities, they united a shrewd policy of making good marriages and large investments in land. Estates and castles, out-of-town houses and coats of arms granted them by the pope, or else by one of the European sovereigns who owed them vast amounts of money, very soon enabled them to forget their origins, often very humble, and embrace the aristocratic way

58

of life, becoming part of the late-mediaeval early-modern process of re-feudalization. Never as in the Florence of the "people" or of the "bourgeois" were there so many tournaments and emblems and heraldic devices.

On the other hand, if the solidarity of the oligarchy made up of the great families (who nonetheless fought like tigers among themselves for supreme power) had sheltered Florentine society from institutional changes brought about "from below," there remained the vast problem of transforming the city-state into a territorial state. In late mediaeval Italy this problem became the basis of a whole new political equilibrium, with the erasure of dozens and dozens of small local governments — which in some cases survived perhaps in form if not in substance — in favour of the gradual annexation of small states into larger and more logical units. This is why northern Italy came to be partitioned between the Duchy of Milan and the Republic of Venice. Much the same thing is true of Florence, whose territory in the early 12th century did not extend beyond the Valdelsa and the Mugello, and did not even include Fiesole, which was just "at the top of the hill." By conducting a ruthless policy of alternating alliances, of the acquisition of territories and the founding of new centres (the *"terrenove"* or New Lands, such as San Giovanni Valdarno, Firenzuola, Scarperia), Florence by the end of the 15th century had in one way or another subdued almost all of northern and central Tuscany, including the cities of Prato, Pistoia, Arezzo, Cortona, Volterra and even Pisa herself, defeated in 1406 after a long siege. One city to escape from the ambitions of the Florentines was Lucca, for all political manoeuvres and military campaigns aimed at gaining control of the city had failed, and Lucca was still at the head of a republic stretching from the Valdinievole to the Lunigiana and southern Garfagnana. The other was Siena, mistress of a large if somewhat sparsely populated territory extending from the Chianti hills to Monte Amiata and from the Maremma to Chiusi, including the important town of Grosseto and the port of Talamone, from which the Sienese for

59

58. Giorgio Vasari: Lorenzo the Magnificent enlarges the city of Florence, detail of the city. Florence, Palazzo Vecchio.

59. Giorgio Vasari: Portrait of Lorenzo the Magnificent. Florence, Uffizi.

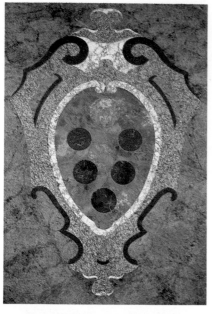

60

61

60. *The Medici coat-of-arms. Florence, San Lorenzo, Chapel of the Princes.*

61. *Justus Utens: Lunette with the Pitti Palace, detail. Florence, Museo di Firenze com'era.*

a long time vainly attempted to organize their independent maritime policy.

Government by an overlord only began in Florence in 1434, when the group of oligarchical families led by the rich and powerful bankers of the Medici family and with ample support from the more modest strata of society, succeeded in defeating and to a large extent exiling the rival group, led by the Albizzi family. However, the head of the Medici family and firm, Cosimo the Elder, never took on the outward trappings of an overlord. He continued to govern the city, as the phrase goes, "from the back of his shop," which was in fact the splendid palace in Via Larga (now Via Cavour) which he had had built by Michelozzo and from which he controlled the affairs of the family, the family firm and the city. Cosimo always refused official posts and honours, contenting himself with checking on the electoral lists and giving his own apparently modest personal advice to the rulers of the city, as well as to foreign ambassadors. But in reality, though clad in the garb of an affable merchant, his authority was no less felt than that of a Duke of Milan or Marquis of Ferrara, girded as they were with military splendours. After the brief paranthesis of his son Piero, who was an invalid, his work was continued by his grandson Lorenzo, known as "the Magnificent." Lorenzo to a large extent abandoned the principle of outward reserve, and, especially in the last years of his government, openly adopted the stance of a real prince. Lorenzo was celebrated for his political and diplomatic acumen — Francesco Guicciardini described him as the "pointer of the scales" in the balance of power of 15th-century Italy — and also for his patronage of artists. In fact the years of his government (1469-1492) coincide with the most splendid and creative period of the early Renaissance in Florence. But we should not turn a blind eye to his more negative side: a really harsh policy, both towards his internal enemies and to those parts of Tuscany subject to Florence; the constant subordination of the interests of the republic to those of his own house and banking enterprises; and a political and financial policy that was far from prudent, and brought the state and the Medici bank to the verge of crisis.

And in fact in 1492, when Lorenzo died, black clouds were looming over Florence. The city was stricken by new outbreaks of conflict between the factions, Charles VIII of France swept down into the country, there was the brief but intense and significant dictatorship of Gerolamo Savonarola from 1494 to 1498, and the subjected cities (such as Pisa in 1494 and Arezzo in 1502) rebelled against Florentine rule. In the wars between France and Spain, which took place in Italy, Florentine dominance in Tuscany appeared to crumble, while Florence herself seemed unable to decide between the Medici family supported from without (what had been a family of bankers now provided two great Renaissance popes, Leo X and Clement VII) and republican forces stemming from an aristocracy that was by now politically enfeebled.

62

THE MEDICI GRAND DUCHY

The siege of Florence in 1530, conducted by the troops of the emperor Charles V on the request of Clement VII, who was anxious to get his own family back into power in the city, was the last great period of republican and "Savonarolian" Florence, symbolized for us by the efforts made by Michelangelo to prepare the fortifications of the city. In accord with the neo-feudal appearance which the Hapsburg empire was giving if not to European politics at least to its outward forms, Florence and its territory, where the disappointed hope of freedom in the early years of the century and the weakness of the city itself had caused a number of fits and starts, had been patiently and laboriously reorganized, and was now raised to the status of duchy and assigned to Cosimo I, who descended from a cadet branch of the Medici. It was the new duke who in the years 1555-1559 managed to realize the ancient dream of Florence: in a long and bitter military campaign he subdued the entire Republic of Siena. Siena was unable to withstand the combined strength of the duke and the Spanish, who had placed Tuscany under their direct vigilance by creating a garrison state thick with fortresses from the promontory of the Argentario to the south coast of Elba. But the City of the Virgin had no intention of giving way easily to its age-old enemy, and Cosimo personally had to accept the union of the two ducal crowns of Florence and Siena, formally independent of each other. Tuscan unity became a constitutional reality only later, in 1559, when pope Pius V conferred on the duke the title of Grand Duke of Florence and Siena.

With Cosimo I the structures of the Tuscan state gradually came into line with what was the great political fact of the 16th century: absolute monarchy. The court became the centre of the grand duchy, while the whole of Tuscany — thanks to a vast programme of princely building, of villas, palaces and fortresses — changed into a kind of extension of the court itself. Cosimo and his successors also saw to the political enfeeblement of the Florentine

63

62. Giorgio Vasari: The Conquest of Pisa, detail. Florence, Palazzo Vecchio.

63. The port of Livorno, built by the Medici.

64

64. *Giambologna: Equestrian statue of Cosimo I. Florence, Piazza della Signoria.*

nobility, whom they loaded with titles while removing not only the least aspiration in politics, but even in the business world which had at one time constituted their strength. From then on the aristocratic world of Tuscany became one of peaceful landowners, who derived safe incomes from the system of share-cropping and the division of the estates into farms, while they viewed the fact of living in contact with the soil as the basic sign of their nobility.

The grand dukes, though they went on living in Florence, and indeed endowed it with a series of great monuments, were not really fond of their capital; nor did they ever succeed in making themselves particularly popular there. For them, however, this was not a disadvantage. Since Florence had for centuries been disliked by the rest of Tuscany, which was justified in identifying it with the forces which in the 14th and 15th centuries had deprived it of its freedom, the Medici understood that the essential basis of their political image would have to be to promote themselves as the princes of the entire region, and not just of the Florentines. Therefore with their presence and with the public works which were their representatives they set about laying stress, here there and everywhere, on their shrewd and provident grand ducal authority. They formed special privileged relationships with several important centres such as Pisa, which enjoyed a new flowering during the 16th century, or the port of Livorno, which thanks to the foundation in 1561 of the Order of the Knights of St. Stephen became the centre of military and maritime activities to defend the coast against the Barbary corsairs, but which at the same time was a "free port." It soon grew to great prosperity, and traditionally provided an exile for the victims of despotic régimes throughout Europe, such as the Jews expelled from Spain or the Calvinists who had to leave France as a result of the revocation of the Edict of Nantes.

After a difficult period coinciding with the reign of Cosimo's son Francesco I (1574-87), during which Tuscany faced a rather severe economic crisis and a widespread outbreak of banditry, the great policies of Cosimo I were continued by his other son, the Grand Duke Ferdinando I (1587-1609). He it was who was really responsible for the economic launching of the port of Livorno, and he guided Florentine commerce and the textile trade (by now centred on the manufacture of silk) towards a new period of prosperity. Ferdinando can also take credit for having slackened the traditional ties of alliance with Spain, which had become too heavy a political burden, and which Cosimo had already attempted to reduce, and for turning instead to France, thereby taking up one of the threads of the policy of mediaeval Florence.

The 17th century brought Tuscany a certain number of problems, as it did to the rest of Europe. War raged more or less everywhere, and it may be that one of the keys to understanding the attachment of the Tuscan people to the grand-ducal family was simply the fact that it managed to keep the region free from the scourge of war. But it could not shelter Tuscany from other troubles, such as the long economic crisis that badly hit the textile

industry, still convalescent after its recovery at the end of the 16th century, or the plague of 1630 which decimated the population. The free port of Livorno remained flourishing, but its cosmopolitan middle class was dominated by the two great economic and maritime powers of the century, the Dutch and the English, so that the Tuscans could derive little benefit from it. Especially with Cosimo III (1670-1723) and Gian Gastone (1723-37), the grand-ducal dynasty seemed to have fallen into a kind of lethargy, not unlike that of the Tuscan aristocracy as a whole, converted into a nobility of farmers.

65. Torello Moricci: View of Florence in the 19th century. Florence, Museo di Firenze Com'era.

66. Gian Gastone, the last of the Medici, who died in 1737. Florence, Uffizi.

THE LORRAINE GRAND DUCHY

The Medici dynasty died out with Gian Gastone, and in the general rearrangements of European institutions following the War of the Polish Succession the grand duchy was assigned to Francis Stephen of Lorraine, husband of the empress Maria Teresa of Hapsburg. But he lived nearly the whole time in Vienna, governing the region through a council of regents. Things went quite differently when, in 1765, he was succeeded by his son Pietro Leopoldo I, who governed directly and vigorously until he was recalled to Vienna in 1790 to ascend the throne of the Empire. The strength of purpose of a prince extraordinarily open to reform was echoed by an intellectual environment in which the rationalistic scientific legacy of Galileo was still alive, and in which circulated the physiocratic theories which had their chief motive force in the Accademia dei Georgofili. An indication of this interest in innovation is the fact that the French *Encyclopédie*, that out-and-out manifesto of the Enlightenment in Europe, was published twice in Tuscany, in 1758 in Lucca and in 1770 in Livorno. Leopoldo carried out a policy of limiting or suppressing the feudal privileges thitherto held by the aristocracy and many ecclesiastical institutions, he put the state finances on a new

67

67. *Pietro Leopoldo of Lorraine with his family. Florence, Museo degli Argenti, Pitti Palace.*

footing, and he laboured to revive agriculture, the meagre yields from which were a problem that increased with the intense population growth which started in the mid-18th century. In this context vast reclamation schemes were undertaken in Val di Chiana, the Pisan plain, the Sienese Maremma and the Valdinievole, while laws were passed to allow the free circulation of grain. Plans were drawn up to sell or long-lease the grand-ducal possessions and those of the privileged institutions. The aim of these last two measures was to enlarge and reinforce the class of small landowners and to broaden the base of the urban and rural middle classes. Issued in 1768 was a new Penal Code largely inspired by the ideas of reform then circulating in Europe. Nor did ecclesiastical life go unchanged, both with the suppression of the courts of the Inquisition and various fiscal privileges of the clergy, and by encouraging a kind of religious reform put forward by the Jansenists in Tuscany.

The departure of the Grand Duke to ascend the throne of the Holy Roman Empire in 1790 produced a considerable movement of discontent. Increasingly connected to the alarming news coming from France, in 1799 (after the French invasion of Italy) this movement led to the formation of the traditionalist faction known as "Viva Maria." Brought into the Napoleonic system in 1801, the grand duchy first became the Kingdom of Etruria under the dynasty of the Bourbons of Parma, and then — from 1807 on — a department of the French Empire. Under Napoleon the projects started during the period of Leopoldo came to fruition, though accompanied by strong new administrative centralization and a series of severe, and in many cases brutal, plunders and forced annulments of old institutions and ancient traditions.

When the Bonapartist adventure came to an end, the Restoration brought the Grand Duke Ferdinando II back to the throne, while the Garrison States and the Principality of Piombino were annexed to the grand duchy. The year 1847 saw the annexation also of the duchy of Lucca, so that the first half of the 19th century substantially saw the completion of regional unity. Though remaining outside the great social and economic changes that during the same period altered the face of Lombardy and Piedmont, Tuscany travelled slowly and cautiously along the road of progress, retaining most of the reforms brought in under Pietro Leopoldo and Napoleon and remaining faithful to a tradition of moderation and tolerance that permitted the development of important cultural initiatives animated by liberal tendencies, such as the scientific and literary "*Gabinetto*" founded by Giovan Pietro Vieusseux and the "*Antologia Vieusseux*," a magazine which between 1821 and 1833 prepared the educated Tuscan public for the idea that the grand-ducal régime should gradually change into a constitutional monarchy. This had, in any case, been a project of Pietro Leopoldo's.

In 1847-48 it was moderate public opinion that led the struggle that ended in the issuing of the Statute in February 1848 and the brief military campaign against Austria in alliance with the Piedmontese. Grand Duke Leopoldo II, though he was beginning to worry about the final outcome of the movement which had thus been started, remained loyal to the agreements he had made with the most determined group of moderates led by Baron Bettino Ricasoli. But in October 1848 events overwhelmed even Tuscany, where as a result of violent protests especially in Livorno and Florence the power was taken over by a revolutionary triumvirate composed of Montanelli, Guerrazzi and Mazzoni, whose immediate aim was to call an Italian constituent assembly and to join up with the Roman republic. In the meanwhile, in February 1849, the grand duke had abandoned Florence for Gaeta.

Leopoldo returned to Florence on July 28th of that year, when the situation caused by the revolutionary years of 1848-49 had already crumbled. In the grand duchy there were neither vendettas nor repressions, but the sovereign repealed the Statute and once again became an absolute monarch, preferring to govern with the aid of military support from Austria. But in spite of all this the last decade of the grand-ducal régime was inspired by the customary sense of moderation. In the meanwhile, moderate thinking people in Tuscany were swinging over to Cavour's ideas of the unity of Italy, while there was also the fear that the end of the Hapsburg-Lorraine régime, written on the wall by this time, would bring with it all kinds of social upheaval. The insurrection of April 1859 and the plebiscite concerning the annexation of Tuscany to Piedmont, both of them incited by the middle classes and aristocracy won over to the cause of a united monarchy of Italy, brought this annexation into being. Six years later, in 1865, the need arose to move the capital of the Kingdom of Italy away from Turin, which was geographically too marginal with regard to the rest of the country, as well as being too obviously linked to the dynastic continuity of a single family, the Savoias, who had to work hard to show that they did not consider Italy as a whole as being annexed to Piedmont! At the same time there was a wish to shift the capital nearer to what on many sides was hoped to be the future capital, which is to say Rome. Along with the fact that it was considered the historical and cultural "capital" of the country, this led to the decision to make Florence the political capital of the new State. And so it remained until 1870, and it was during this period or shortly after that the city was in part demolished and modernized in ways that to a certain degree deformed its traditional design, but which were at that time thought necessary to give it the outward appearance of a great modern city.

68

68. Demonstration in favour of Italian unity in front of Palazzo Vecchio. Florence, Museo di Firenze com'era.

The Medici Villas

At the end of the 16th century the Flemish painter Justus Utens made 14 lunettes for the Medici villa of Artimino, each one depicting a house in the region belonging to the granducal family. As a number of these great villas have been subjected to remodelling and alterations that have profoundly changed their character, while others have completely disappeared, these lunettes by Utens (now in the "Firenze com'era" museum in Florence) are a valuable source of information.

The villas, with their parklands, were scattered throughout the territory of the State, in such a way that the sovereign could move to any part of it and yet remain, as it were, at home. Still existing today are: Cafaggiolo in the Mugello, on the road to the Futa pass (and it is something of a "mother house" for the Medici); the villa of Trebbio nearby; Poggio a Caiano near Pistoia, designed in 1485 by Giuliano da Sangallo; Castello, between Florence and Sesto on the Prato road; Seravezza, built by Cosimo I near the marble quarries and silver mines in which he took a personal interest; La Petraia, which was severely remodelled in the 19th century, when Florence became the capital and the villa became a royal residence; Palazzo Pitti in Florence, with the great complex of the Boboli Gardens and the Fortezza del Belvedere; Lappeggi near Grassina, south of Florence, now much modified and spoilt; La Magia near Quarrata, in the area of Monte Albano; Marignolle; L'Ambrogiana at Montelupo, now a nursing home for the mentally disturbed; Montevettolini on the slopes of Monte Albano; Colle Salvetti; Artimino. Lost to us is the villa of Pratolino, with its marvellous park (of which a few monuments remain).

I

II

III

V

V

I. *Justus Utens: The Medici Villa of Trebbio.*

II. *A joust taking place in front of a Medici Villa.*

IV-V. *The Villa of Cafaggiolo in Utens's lunette and as it is today.*

III. *The Villa at Poggio a Caiano.*

69

69. Art Nouveau architecture. Florence.

TUSCANY AS PART OF THE ITALIAN WORLD

Following unification the country underwent a gradual process of transformation. The wool industry of Prato, the shipyards of Livorno, the mines of Elba, the steelworks of Piombino and the numerous ironworks of Florence and Pistoia, were all giving it a new, more modern and more dynamic appearance. Already begun under the grand duchy, the railway network was being extended, while the traditional resources of the region — the land, and its special products, wine and oil — still anchored to the share-cropping system, inevitably generated social and mental conservatism. The ruling classes continued to be moderate, with a more "clerical" tendency in the Lucchesia and a more free-thinking (or "Massonic") one in Florence and Livorno, where there was no lack of democratic and republican feeling. The growing labour movement was at first influenced by the ideas of Bakunin, but then became socialist not only in Florence, Livorno and Piombino, but also in smaller centres such as Empoli and Colle Val d'Elsa, while among the marble quarrymen of the Carrara area there grew up a tendency to anarchy which has become traditional to them.

The local governments at that time were for the most part democratic-liberal, often making use of implicit support from the Catholics, though here and there were discernible signs of the growth of the socialist movement, the strength of which would be seen later on with the introduction of universal suffrage, while the deep-rooted Catholicism of the people gave vent to its feelings through the organization of the so-called "white" leagues of workers.

The early 20th century, especially in Florence, was marked by furious warfare between intellectuals and newspapers with various views, some of which soon became well-known or notorious throughout the nation. Examples are Papini and Prezzolini's "La Voce," Corradini's "Il Regno" and Salvemini's "L'Unità." Battles were continuous and violent, with their epicentre in the "salon" frequented by militant writers and artists, the "Caffè delle Giubbe Rosse" in the Piazza della Repubblica in Florence: the very place where the Mercato Vecchio, the "Old Market," stood before so much of the city was demolished to create a more modern political image. And then, Florence can lay claim to being the birthplace of the Futurist movement in painting, while on another plane it was often the scene of furious diatribes (which often came to blows) between "interventionists" and "neutralists" at the outbreak of the First World War.

As in the rest of Italy, the immediate post-war years threw Tuscany into a critical period worsened by the fact that the war itself had temporarily concealed such problems as unemployment, and with the "wartime economy" had given rise to a whole series of industries which were bound either to be abolished or be drastically cut down with the coming of peace. Discontent was soon transformed into strikes, the occupation of factories and protests in the streets, backed now by the "white" and now by

70

the "red" leagues. And in fact it was in opposition to these two factions that in 1920-22 Fascism emerged, taking on the two faces (destined to remain quite distinct from one another, and sometimes on opposite sides) of reaction from the agrarian community on the one hand, and on the other the brutal, nihilistic behaviour of the Fascist "squads," with their more or less republican aims and their irreverence towards the clergy. Fascism was caught between its objective stance of being against the workers and its deep-rooted prejudice against the middle classes.

Between 1922 and 1925 the more brutally eversive side of Fascism died down, as the movement had become legitimized by an established régime that was obliged to repress its most arbitrary and violent features. But the political debate was not altogether silenced. The Livorno Congress of 1921 saw the foundation of the Italian Communist Party, and no sooner had the government made Mussolini the "legitimate" dictator of the country than the first anti-Fascist newspaper was founded, and in no other city than Florence. This was "Non Mollare," edited by Carlo Rosselli, Gaetano Salvemini, Ernesto Rossi and Piero Calamandrei.

As far as the Fascist régime was concerned, it found Florence a hard place to deal with, even among its own most fervent supporters. Within the Fascist party in Florence there were many with republican and libertarian views, and we need only mention one person of such stature as Ardengo Soffici. If Fascism was to get a grip on Tuscany it had not only to show its face of repression, but also the other one: the face that was in its way

71

71. *Contemporary architecture (Arch. Savioli). Florence.*

the heir of Futurism, an area in which there was room for suggestions for future progress or for attitudes that were at least less forcefully "under control". This gave rise to the sort of social and intellectual tension expressed in papers such as "Il Bargello" and which (partly in response to the crisis of 1929, which particularly hit the industrial and mining sectors) caused the characteristic tendency to launch into vast public works which absorbed manpower and gave an impression of progress and activity. Some results of this were the Firenze-Mare motorway, the direct railway-line from Florence to Bologna, and a number of buildings which for a long time remained exemplary of their kind, such as the Santa Maria Novella railway station in Florence. The Tuscan "capital" was also the scene of continuous artistic and cultural experimentation on the part of the régime, with a wealth of ideas some of which were fairly non-conformist, especially when the Florentine Alessandro Pavolini became Minister of "Popular Culture."

The Second World War, and particularly the terrible years of 1944-45, hit Tuscany extremely hard, partly because the territory was split in two by the so-called "Gothic Line", the heavily fortified line from Pisa to Rimini which the Germans were determined to hold. During the summer of 1944 the allied advance was very slow, while the population was subjected to considerable hardship, and there was much damage from bombing and artillery fire. At the same time there were some ugly episodes of repression and on certain occasions downright barbarity, such as deportations, mass shootings and indiscriminate slaughters such as that of the Fucecchio swamps or at Sant'Anna di Stazzema. However, even in such sad and dramatic times the character of the Tuscans (factious perhaps, but also courageous) had a chance to reveal itself. The Resistance was not only and not principally a matter of groups of partisans, but a kind of spontaneous movement on the part of the people, shown by hiding fugitives and wanted persons, helping the homeless and refugees, and putting up resistance, albeit passive, to the harsh measures imposed by the forces of occupation.

As we have seen, the post-war reconstruction once more placed Tuscany in the vanguard of Italy and Europe as a land of culture and economic activities directed not merely at development in terms of quantity, but also at safeguarding traditions and quality. Even agriculture, which in the immediate post-war years was perhaps rather too neglected in the name of the aprioristic need for "progress" in terms of industrialization, has for some time now been regaining its normal role in the region. This, however, has been achieved with the aid of the most advanced techniques and the determination to improve the level of the produce, so as to find a place for Tuscan wines and olive oil, for example, in a world market that is becoming more and more sophisticated and demanding.

Hypergothic and Hyperexotic

Among so many things one comes to Tuscany to find things mediaeval. And indeed one finds them often, in cities, in villages and out in the country, set among hills and cypresses. But take care! Those battlements, those lovely towers, those embrasures and double-lighted windows, may conceal a fake. Usually, the more mediaeval a thing looks the less likely it is to be so.

The Romantic age and the later neo-Gothic period, along with the eclectic and decadent taste of the turn of the century, filled Tuscany with fakes, follies and faithless restorations. This does not of course mean that many of these buildings are not very beautiful, and have much artistic merit of their own, and are works of art or at least monuments of interest, bearing precious witness to the taste of a certain epoch. It is just that they have nothing to do with the Middle Ages, or even with a correct philological and archeological approach to them.

In Via Calimala in Florence you find the "Palagio dell'Arte della Lana" (Palace of the Wool Guild), the nucleus of which dates from the very early 15th century; but in 1905 Enrico Lusini "restored" it in a manner that is just too "mediaeval" for words. In the outskirts of Florence, on the road up to Fiesole from Ponte a Mensola, is the ancient castle of Vincigliata, a Visdomini property already in existence in the 11th century. But it was remodelled in neo-mediaeval style by Giuseppe Fancelli in 1855-65. Brolio, Strozzavolpe near Poggibonsi, and even the town centre of San Gimignano have had a good few coats of 19th-century mediaeval paint.

Nor did the neo-Gothic satisfy a certain number of eccentric spirits, and these preferred to go in for the Exotic. The Villa di Sammezzano, near Pontassieve in the Valdarno, is a kind of phoney Alhambra, while on the Porrettana near Rioli (between 1850 and 1896) Cesare Mattei had a fairytale castle built for him. A jumble of styles, with plenty of echoes of Moorish and Russian, it is called La Rocchetta, and may be viewed as a sort of Tusco-Emilian Neuschwanstein. And indeed among its guests were Ludwig II of Bavaria and Elizabeth of Hapsburg, wife of Franz Joseph.

I. Palagio dell'Arte della Lana, Florence.

II. The Villa di Sammezzano.

III. A castle built in neo-mediaeval style near Florence.

IV. The castle of Vincigliata.

I

II

III

IV

72

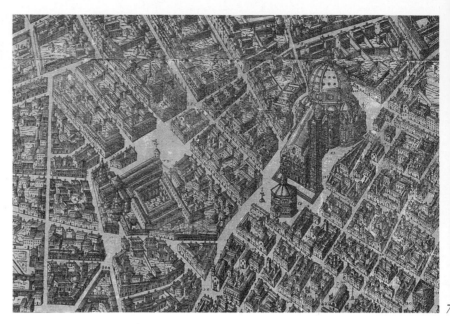

7

72. *The centre of Florence in an aerial view.*

73. *Stefano Bonsignori: Map of Florence in 1584, detail. Florence, Uffizi, Collection of Prints and Drawings.*

INVITATION TO THE JOURNEY
WHERE CAN WE START FROM?

Let us at random take any Italian or foreign tourist who wishes to visit Tuscany, an undertaking which if confronted with passable seriousness will take him at least a fortnight, whether he does it by train and bus, in his Toyota or thumbing lifts. The first problem he faces is: how to enter the region? What side should one besiege Tuscany from?

The idea of starting from Florence, given the city's central position in the region, and branching out from there on excursions of one or more days, makes sense if our tourist flies to Pisa airport (the only decent one in Tuscany) and takes the shuttle-service by rail. In little more than an hour he will find himself opposite the apse of Santa Maria Novella. But otherwise?

There we have the question "where does Tuscany begin?" The Etruscans first saw the coastline, coming from the sea — on the assumption that they did in fact arrive that way. But today one is rather unlikely to come in from the sea. Is there any "special" route to assure us of an enjoyable and profitable journey?

Before answering, and before we set off, it would be as well to set down a few facts. The road network of the region is considerable, with nearly 20,000 kilometers of roads, apart from more than 300 km of motorways. The latter comprise the A1 (Autostrada del Sole), the A12 (Tirrenica or Autostrada dei Fiori) the A11 (the Firenze-Mare opened in 1933, one of the earliest of its kind in Europe) and the A15 (della Cisa) which runs along the valley of the Magra, connecting the A12 with the A1. A series of "superstrade" radiate from these. Well known, for example, is the Florence-Siena-Grosseto link, joining the Autostrada del Sole to south-western Tuscany, while in the Val di Chiana there is another motorway leading to Umbria and the Adriatic. Almost abandoned

74. *The Cathedral of Florence and Giot-*
to's Belltower.

75

7

75. *Detail of the outside of the Baptistry, Florence.*

76. *Detail of the decoration inside the Baptistry.*

77. *The facade of the church of Santa Maria Novella, Florence.*

78. *Masaccio: Holy Trinity. Florence, Santa Maria Novella.*

79. *Giotto: Death of Saint Francis, detail. Florence, Santa Croce, Bardi Chapel.*

today is the Strada Statale 2, the glorious Via Cassia, mostly used by local traffic, while long-distance drivers prefer the A1. This is a pity, for it is a beautiful road, passing through enchanting landscapes and towns abounding in art and history. On the other hand Strada Statale 1, the Via Aurelia, still poses a big problem. This is the ancient Roman road and the only main coastal road south of Pisa, and work has gone on for years to supply it with at least a dual carriageway. But many stretches are still without one, which makes it dangerous and nearly always packed with traffic in the summer months. We should mention that Tuscany has a dense and efficient network of bus services, which tourists seldom know about or use as much as they might.

In tune with a general tendency due to the growth of road traffic, both public and private, the development of the railways has come to a halt. The region has less than 1400 km of railway lines, of which barely more than half are electrified. Anyone who has travelled in Italy, be he Tuscan or otherwise, is familiar with the two main lines: the Turin-Rome line along the coast and the Milan-Rome inland route. But a tourist with a liking for revivals and enough time, patience and imagination, might think of taking some lesser line, such as the "trenino" from Borgo San Lorenzo to Faenza, or the Pisa-Cècina-Volterra line, or yet again the one (under private management) from Arezzo to Pratovecchio and Stia. He would find himself in contact with a different Tuscany, with glimpses of a landscape seldom seen and hardly even guessed

77

78

79

80

81

80. The Old Sacristy. Florence, San Lorenzo.

81. Palazzo Vecchio, Florence.

at, old skills and technologies still in use, and a sense of time and human relations quite different from what one is used to in the big cities or along the main roads. But maybe this advice is best offered to a special kind of traveller: one who travels less to discover places than to discover himself.

Of the airports it is better not to speak. We have no wish to get bogged down in arguments about whether or not they are needed. We need only say that there are none, except the one at Pisa, and even this is used chiefly for internal flights. It is now efficiently connected to Florence by rail, and though it has been often urged that the "capital" should have its own international airport, present conditions do not appear to justify such a thing.

On the other hand the situation regarding ports is not too bad. In addition to the great port of Livorno there is that of Piombino, rather smaller but nonetheless important for the local steel industry and communications with the island of Elba. Carrara and Viareggio both have fair-sized ports, while Vada, Baratti, Castiglione della Pescaia, Talamone, Porto Ercole and Porto Santo Stefano are little harbours for fishing and tourism. Portoferraio, important before the war because of the many industrial plants (since destroyed) has now regained some measure of vitality thanks chiefly to tourism.

This is not a tourist guide, nor can it in any way replace guides, maps and so on. All the same, setting out to be a vademecum for the tourist who has no intention of going mad or joining the mob,

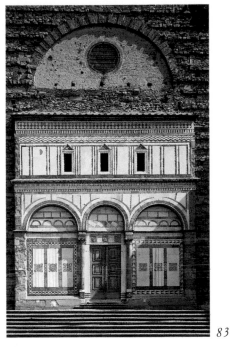

82. *The facade of San Miniato al Monte, Florence.*

83. *The facade of Badia Fiesolana. Florence, San Domenico di Fiesole.*

it too will forward a choice of routes. And for convenience and more logical presentation we will proceed as far as possible in the directions that seem most natural to the modern western mind, which is to say from north to south and from west to east. Bearing in mind, above all, that the good traveller is a sage. He does not allow himself to be carried away by the desire to see everything, he does not tear his hair if he misses some objective that has three asterisks in his guidebook. When he feels the need he does not deny himself the pleasure of a swift gallop, a trip taken all in one breath, without ever leaving the window of a train or the wheel of a car. Such journeys do not enable him to pause over details, but give him the feeling and as it were the "aroma" of a region. Nor, on the other hand, will he deny himself the luxury of deviating from his route, of making unforeseen incursions, of "wasting" an afternoon sipping a glass of wine, or watching the sun go down over the vineyards of Chianti or, in the Maremma, over the sea. Anyone unwilling to do at least one of these things would do better not to come travelling in Tuscany. In fact, he would do better not to travel at all.

84

85

86

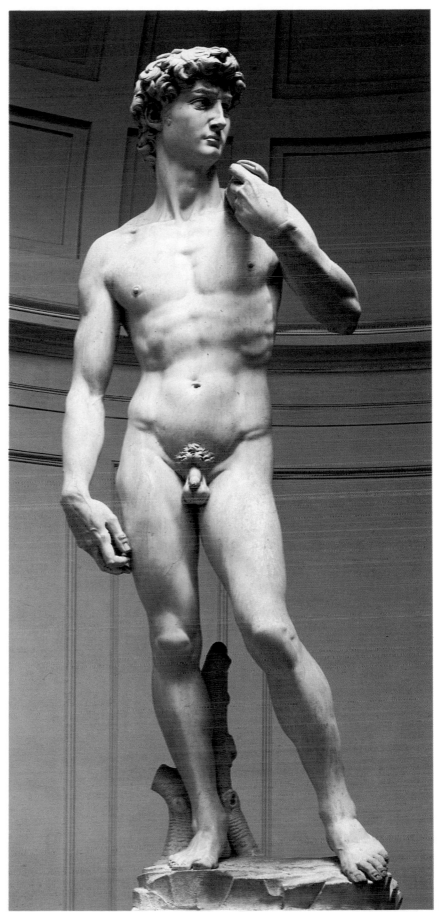

84. *The Arno at Ponte Santa Trinita, Florence.*

85. *Via Toscanella, in the area of Santo Spirito, Florence.*

86. *A fountain called Fontana dell'Oceano in the Boboli Gardens, Florence.*

87. *Donatello: Bronze David. Florence, National Museum of the Bargello.*

88. *Michelangelo: David. Florence, Academy.*

THE LUNIGIANA AND VERSILIA

89

89. *Mount Tambura and some of the quarries in the Apuan Alps.*

Rather than taking the A15 motorway, which passes under the Cisa in a tunnel, the tourist would be well advised to come from Emilia by S.S. (Strada Statale) 62, perhaps after stopping off in Berceto, where he can taste the best mushrooms in the district. In this way he will cross the ancient pass, sacred to pilgrims on their way from France to Rome, and will traverse the Lunigiana, which is the valley of the Magra (the last reaches of which are, however, in Liguria, between La Spezia and Sarzana). The first important centre to the south of the Cisa Pass is Pontrèmoli, mentioned for the first time in 990 A.D. as a staging-post on the Via Francigena, and also traditionally important as a centre for the travelling booksellers of central Italy. For this latter reason the "Bancarella" Prize is awarded here annually (*bancarella* = bookstall). At the meeting of the Magra and its tributary the Verde, the old town has retained its slate roofs and its tiny fields along the river banks which are features of the Lunigiana. Continuing south, we pass beneath the village of Filattiera, where we can visit a (restored) Malaspina castle on the left of the river, but almost opposite, on the right, we advise a short deviation to visit Mulazzo, a Malaspina castle where Dante found hospitality in 1306. Other castles built by the Malaspina family can be seen as we go down river, at Villafranca, Lusuolo and Monti, near where the Taverone flows into the Magra. If we turn up the Taverone we will find still more castles (Pontebosio, Licciana Nardi, Bastia); or else we can go on to Aulla, and make a deviation from there to visit the fortresses of Fosdinovo and Podenzana.

At Aulla the tourist has two possible routes. If he takes S.S. 445 he will enter the upper valley of the Serchio, which is to say the Garfagnana, visiting Castelnuovo, Barga and Bagni di Lucca. Thence he will follow the valley to the east of the Apuan Alps and reach Lucca by way of S.S. 12. The second route, along S.S. 62, will lead him to Sarzana, where he can join the Via Aurelia as far as Massa, and reach Lucca and Pisa from there. In either case his journey is overshadowed by the massif of the Apuan Alps.

The remains of Luni, on the border between the present regions of Liguria and Tuscany, are now sandwiched between the A12 motorway and the Via Aurelia. A Roman colony near the mouth of the Magra and important for its trade in Apuan marble, it began to decline in the 4th century, largely on account of malaria, and in the late Middle Ages was several times sacked by the Saracens and the Normans. In 1204 the bishop's Curia was once and for all transferred to Sarzana. Apart from an interesting archaeological museum, worth looking at today remain the ruins of the amphitheatre and the cathedral. Between Sarzana and Luni, with short deviations, we get to Castelnuovo Magra, with splendid views over the Gulf of La Spezia and a parish church containing an Ascent to Calvary, attributed to Breugel, and the fortress of Fosdinovo.

Carrara is the "capital" of the marble industry. Quarrying has been going on here for two thousand years, and some three hundred quarries are still working. Things to visit here are the Duomo (cathedral), the façade of which is Romanesque, and faced with stripes of grey and white marble in the Pisan style, though the building as a whole only dates from the 14th century; the 16th-century Accademia delle Belle Arti, once the palace of the Cybo Malaspina family, rulers of the city; and the Baroque church of the Madonna delle Grazie. From Carrara one can make a number of excursions to the marble quarries and to panoramic viewpoints in the Apuan Alps. The present layout of Carrara is modern, with some interesting echoes of neoclassicism. Massa, on the other hand, is distinguished by a mediaeval nucleus dominated by the recently restored fortress (a mediaeval nucleus on which in the 15th and 16th centuries the Malaspina erected their Renaissance residence) and a 16th-century layout centred around Piazza degli Aranci, over which towers the Palazzo Cybo Malaspina (now the Prefecture).

It is from Massa, or rather from Seravezza just to the south-east, that the most beautiful excursions may be taken into the Apuan Alps, amid chestnut woods and really high peaks such as the Sumbra (1764 metres) and Pania della Croce (1858 metres), which owing to the Apuan marble, appear to be snow-covered even when they are not. A road with wonderful views crosses the Apuan massif, leading on the far side to Castelnuovo Garfagnana, where one should pay due homage to the fortress where the great poet Ludovico Ariosto lived when he was delegate of the d'Este government. From here one can bravely start on the climb up S.S. 324 that crosses the Appennines at the breathtaking pass of Foce delle Radici (and on the way down can choose between the opulent Sassuolo, the smiling Frignano or the picturesque mountains around Porretta), or else one can take the road towards Castiglione di Garfagnana, which also leads one to the Passo delle Radici, but by way of San Pellegrino in Alpe where there is an ancient Hospice and a famous sanctuary dating back to the 7th century. The Hospice is now an interesting ethnological museum, containing a wealth of traditional tools of the Garfagnana, a collection well known to students of artisan culture.

If our tourist has a certain sense of nostalgia, and is not put off by kitsch, then an itinerary we can recommend — though not between the months of June and September — is to take the coast road from the mouth of the Magra to that of the Serchio, or the Arno, or even as far as Livorno, where the coast changes entirely in character, becoming high and rocky. The whole stretch can be done on the A12 motorway, or better still on Via Aurelia — and a truly amazing ride it is. For much of the way there are pinewoods on the left-hand side, with the soaring Apuan Alps in the background, while on the right, from Marinella di Sarzana near Luni all the way to Viareggio one is separated from the sea by an uninterrupted series of towns whose names until a few decades ago called up irresistible echoes in literary life and elegant society: Forte dei Marmi, Marina di Pietrasanta, Lido di Camaiore, Viareggio itself. Until this point one can take the coast road (S.S.

90

91

90. *The river Carrione in Carrara, white with marble dust.*

91. *Bathers on the beach at Viareggio.*

92

92. *One of the rooms in the Malaspina Castle, Massa.*

93. *Pieve di Santa Maria at Vicopisano (Pisa).*

9

328), keeping the seaside resorts — a thin strip occupying the entire coastline of Versilia — on the left, and the beach with its bathing establishments on the right. The place-names we come across and the people they bring to mind recall the cultural and social splendours of the early years of the century, with the cafés frequented by fashionable intellectuals. Viareggio, when it is not swamped with thousands of summer bathers or the crowds who come to see the Carnival, is worth a trip in itself. The Viareggio I love best is the Viareggio of late autumn or perhaps even early spring, very likely windswept and lashed with rain, or warmed just faintly ,by a timid sun. It is then that the Art Nouveau architecture and the semi-deserted Edwardian hotels exude all their charm, and it is then that Shelley, D'Annunzio, Puccini and Viani seem to be still there, haunting the Lido of "their" Versilia.

After Viareggio we lose sight of the sea until we get to Marina di Pisa, for we have reached the long series of dense forests that give directly onto the sea, with stretches of Mediterranean scrub mingling with the ancient spell of the pinewoods. We have the maquis of Migliarino, the once-royal (now presidential) estate at San Rossore, Barbaricina with its splendid horses, and then, between Pisa and Livorno, the estates of Tombolo and Coltano, with their sad memories of the war and the years just after it, but preserving some natural scenery that is still wild and intact.

This is also one of the areas which most forcibly reminds us of the times when the low coastlines along the Tyrrhenian Sea were

94.

95.

invaded by marshes. The straight roads between the tall pines, and the youth of the trees themselves, speak of recent planning and rationalization. The stretch between the Serchio and the Arno is alluvial soil and relatively recent, for at one time the mouths of the two rivers were far closer together, and Pisa was a city on the sea.

But between Viareggio and Pisa, before proceeding along beside the maquis of Migliarino, music-lovers will want to pay homage to Giacomo Puccini. From Torre del Lago a treelined avenue leads to the western shore of the Lago di Massaciuccoli, the last remnant of the lagoon formed in prehistoric times by the common delta of the Serchio and the Arno. Eels, tench and pike still live in its shallow waters, while one can still wait in the cane-brakes for the flight of waterbirds. Overlooking the lake is Villa Puccini, containing many souvenirs of the composer, and there every year at the end of the summer they hold the Puccini Festival, one of the operatic events dearest to the hearts of Tuscans.

94. The marshes in the park of San Rossore (Pisa).

95. The beach at San Rossore (Pisa) with pine trees damaged by the saltwater.

96

97

98

96. *Piazza dei Miracoli in Pisa, with the Baptistry, the Cathedral and the Leaning Tower.*

97. *The interior of the Baptistry, Pisa.*

98. *The Camposanto monumentale in Pisa.*

99. *Nicola Pisano: the Pulpit of the Baptistry, Pisa.*

100

101

100. *The ravine called Orrido di Botri in Garfagnana.*

101. *The large Red Stalactite in the Cave of the Wind in Garfagnana.*

THE LUCCHESIA

The journey from Viareggio to Lucca is easy and pleasant. One might, for example, take S.S. 439 across Monte Quiesa, enjoying fine views and good food on the way.

There are, as we said, other ways of reaching Lucca. For example, we can follow the course of the Serchio, which means travelling the length of the Garfagnana. We mentioned just now that both from Aulla and from Massa one can get to the main town of the Garfagnana, Castelnuovo. The roads are very windy and narrow in parts, but the traveller is rewarded by majestic chestnut woods and staggering views of the Apuan Alps and the Appennines. Through country redolent with memories of the poet Giovanni Pascoli, especially at Castelvecchio, S.S. 445 leads to Barga, where there is a splendid cathedral in the Lombard Romanesque style, unfortunately remodelled several times and badly damaged in the earthquake of 1920, but now well restored so that its true nature is once again visible. Near Barga lovers of the Romanesque might at least take a trip to Gallicano to see the façade of the Pieve di Sant'Iacopo. Nature-lovers, on the other hand, would do better to climb the road leading towards the Pania della Croce, at the foot of which is the Grotta del Vento (Cave of the Wind), with its forest of stalactites leading for more than a kilometer into the mountain.

Continuing towards Lucca, and near Fornaci di Barga (where there is a large metal-works), we find Loppia, in the vicinity of which we might visit the 10th-century Pieve di Santa Maria. Further on, crossing to the right bank of the Serchio after the bridge of Calavorno, we can reach the Tuscan equivalent of the Grand Canyon, the Orrido di Botri cut sheer between the mountains, with the Rio Pelago flowing in the bottom and high on its walls the nests of the golden eagle. Then, after Borgo a Mozzano, with its paper-works and its 15th and 16th century churches, there are other possible short deviations from S.S. 12 to visit the 13th-century Pieve di Santa Maria at Diecimo, and the two Romanesque Pievi at Brancoli, San Giorgio and San Lorenzo in Corte (11th-12th centuries). While in Borgo a Mozzano, folklore enthusiasts will not have failed to cast an eye at the Ponte della Maddalena, which may have been built in the 14th century, but which in local legend is called "The Devil's Bridge". What is more, he is said to have built it in a single night. In any case, devils and witches seem really at home in the Garfagnana and Lucchesia, among the Romanesque Pievi and the superb 16th to 18th century country houses built by the aristocracy of Lucca on the profits they made from the silk trade. These "Villas", which are worth a tour on their own, are scattered throughout the territory of Lucca in an area stretching in the north-west from the valley of the Freddana (tributary of the Serchio) in an easterly direction more or less as far as Porcari, half way between Lucca and Montecatini. Out of so many, perhaps the most worth a visit are Villa Torrigiani at Segromigno, Villa Mansi (now Villa Salom) at

103

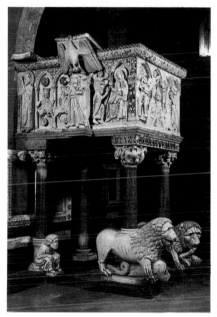

104

Piaggiori, and Villa Reale at Màrlia.

Arriving at Lucca through the Lunigiana or the Garfagnana are two good ways of doing so, unless of course one gets there straight from Florence, which is for obvious reasons the way taken by most tourists, in haste or in groups. Such a traveller will come along the Firenze-Mare motorway, which (we must admit) provides some wonderful glimpses as well as an almost infinite variety of detours towards the Prato area, or that of Pistoia, the thermal baths of Montecatini and Monsummano, and the Valdinievole with the little towns of Pescia and Collodi, and the delightful villages of Borgo a Buggiano and Montecarlo perched on the hilltops. (These were scarcely less than islands in times when between the Pescia and the Arno there was nothing but swamps, the only remainder of which is the marshy flatlands of Fucecchio).

But another interesting way of reaching the Lucchesia from the direction of Emilia is to take S.S. 12 (the Abetone Pass), through the snows which all the skiers in Tuscany have made their first descents and mistakes on. Between one hairpin bend and the next you will come across towns such as Cutigliano and follow the upper reaches of the Lima as far as the vicinity of San Marcello Pistoiese. At this point there are three roads to choose from. Either you turn south-west and follow the S.S. 12 along the Lima valley, arriving at Borgo a Mozzano by way of Bagni di Lucca; or you take the 633 southwards over Monte Serra to the tourist centre of Marliana, and thence to Montecatini and the Valdinievole; or else you head due east, and then turn south for a tough drive along S.S. 66 across the Montagna Pistoiese. In this way you will be able to visit the towns of Gavinana and Maresca, and shortly before Pistoia you will cross the other noble road of the Pistoia mountains, which is S.S. 64, headed for Bologna over the picturesque Passo della Collina and by way of the area between the Sambuca and Porretta Terme. The district is full of artificial lakes and mighty trees, which give it an air of being northern, perhaps in the Baltic, or even in Canada.

102. The village of Colle, near Castelnuovo Garfagnana.

103. The bridge of the Magdalen, called Ponte del Diavolo or Devil's Bridge, at Borgo a Mozzano.

104. The Romanesque pulpit in the Cathedral of Barga.

105

1

106

1

105. *Palazzo Guinigi in Lucca.*

106. *The apse of the church of San Frediano in Lucca.*

107. *The market square, the centre of the old Roman amphitheatre, in Lucca.*

108. *The church and belltower of San Michele in Foro, Lucca.*

109. *Jacopo della Quercia: Tomb of Ilaria del Carretto, detail. Lucca, Cathedral.*

110. *Bonaventura Berlinghieri: Saint Francis and stories from his life. Pescia, San Francesco.*

(following page)
111. *Villa Torrigiani, near Lucca.*

112. *The gardens of Villa Torrigiani.*

113. *Villa Garzoni at Collodi.*

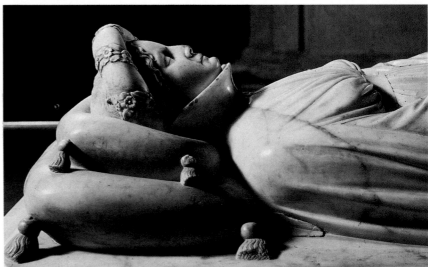

1

111

112

113

Spas and Hot Springs

Spas and hot springs have been cele-brated in Tuscany since Etruscan and Roman times, and were even famous in the Middle Ages, when hydrother-apy was very popular. The best-known watering-place in Tuscany, at least since the 14th century, has been Montecatini, where most of the plants carry out cures of the digestive system by the use of mineral waters. Also important is Chianciano Terme, with its waters that are good for ailments of the liver. Casciana Terme, near Pontedera, is known for its baths and irrigations. Bagni di Lucca (famous in ancient times as the baths of Corsena, and frequented by the high society of Europe throughout the 19th century) offers waters and mud to cure rheu-matism, arthritis and uricaemia. The hydrotherapeutic cures at San Giu-liano Terme, between Lucca and Pisa, are effective for diseases of the bones. San Casciano dei Bagni, near Cetona, and therefore in the vicinity of Chian-ciano, has hot water cures for rheu-matism and diseases of the metabo-lism. Rheumatism and skin diseases are a speciality at Rapolano Terme, between Siena and Val di Chiana. Equi Terme, between Lucca and Aul-la, has radioactive waters used since Roman times with success against chronic diseases of the respiratory sys-tem. Near Amiata there are the pic-turesque Bagno Vignoni (where Lor-enzo the Magnificent went in 1490) and Bagno San Filippo. The Terme di Bagnolo near Follonica treat trauma-tic ailments, arthritis and gout. The same ailments are treated at the Terme di Caldana, which is not far away and can perhaps be identified with the Baths of Populonia men-tioned by ancient writers. The Terme di Saturnia, not far from Sovana, have warm sulphur baths, inhalations and exudative treatments good for trou-bles in the respiratory system. Pope Pius II visited the baths at Petriolo, not far from the Abbey of San Gal-gano, which have sulphurous waters effective in the treatment of trouble with the metabolism, arthritis and gout (it was from this last that the Piccolomini pope sought relief). Mediaeval doctors did not agree on the efficacy of hydrotherapeutic treat-ment, and nor do doctors today. But from Montecatini to Petriolo a thriv-

I. The spas at Montecatini.

II. The spa of Bagno Vignoni.

III. The Terme di Saturnia.

IV. Memmo di Filippuccio: The bath. San Gimignano, Palazzo del Popolo.

 II

III

ing tourist trade has sprung up in the last few decades, and the baths have become equipped to meet the demand. Even if waters and mud only do you a relative amount of good, fresh air and peace are helpful factors in re-gaining one's health.

IV

114

114. The belltower of the church of San Giovanni Maggiore at Borgo San Lorenzo, in the Mugello.

THE APPENNINE ROADS

It is a little sad, this story of the mountain roads and the Appennine passes. We admit that a lot of roads are narrow, pot-holed, steep, a mass of bends, and even quite dangerous, particularly by night or in the winter. But if you flash through Tuscany by way of the Autostrada del Sole, which gives the traveller no time even to realize that there is such a place as the wonderful Mugello on his left, and that plummets down to Prato leaving unnoticed the Monti della Calvana to the right, and to the left the massif which culminates in Monte Morello, well then, this is a region that has been violated without being possessed, and ruined without enjoyment.

What are the alternatives then? For anyone with the time, and the ability to stay calm at the wheel of his car, they are many and various. Let us start from Bologna, and assume that the charms of the Autostrada are no longer so ravishing as once they were. One could take S.S. 325 from Castiglion de' Pepoli to Montepiano, with possible excursions of interest to the 16th-century sanctuary at Boccadirio and the artificial lake of Brasimone. Thereafter one could make one's way down the valley of the Bisenzio, through Vernio and Vaiano (with its 11th-13th century church of San Salvatore) as far as Prato. From here (wishing to avoid the Autostrada) we may reach Florence by way of the Sesto road along the south of Monte Morello, or else by way of Campi, Brozzi and Quaracchi, which follows the course of the Arno and is in fact the lovely "Via Pistoiese" that leads to Poggio a Caiano with its fine Medici villa and to Carmignano, famous for its red wines.

But another way to come from Bologna is by S.S. 65, which leaves Emilia just south of Monghidoro (at Filigara we still see the old customs buildings once at the borders of the Papal States and the grand duchy), crosses the passes of the Raticosa and the Futa, and then falls steeply through the Mugello, touching on the upper reaches of the Sieve and passing near Barberino, which has the fine 15th-century monastery of Bosco ai Frati, the Medici villa of Cafaggiolo and the castle of Trebbio. Once over the Passo di Pratolino and past the splendid park of Villa Demidoff (once a Medici estate) S.S. 65, at least for the Florentines, becomes "Via Bolognese" and arrives in what by now is the centre of Florence at Piazza della Libertà (formerly Piazza San Gallo).

Shortly after passing the castle of Trebbio, the traveller on his way to Florence from the Futa joins up with S.S. 503. This is the road from Firenzuola and the area of "Romagna Toscana" corresponding to the upper valley of the Santerno. It has by now crossed the Passo del Giogo and come down through Scarperia, the Florentine "terranova" that boasts such a fine Town Hall, and San Piero a Sieve, where there is an impressive Medici fortress.

Through the upper valley of the Santerno one can also reach the Mugello if one comes from Imola. But, either from Imola or Faenza, another route into Tuscany is through the valley of the Sènio by way of Castagno (birthplace of the famous painter,

Andrea del Castagno, 1423-57), past Badia di Susinana and Palazzuolo and over the pass of the Sambuca. Shortly after that the road joins the one coming down from the Val di Làmone through the important town of Marradi. From this point we have no trouble in reaching Borgo San Lorenzo, the historic centre of the Mugello. This is the meeting point of the roads coming over from Romagna, by way of San Benedetto and the pass of the Muraglione. San Benedetto dell'Alpe is mentioned by Dante, with its waterfall which he compares with the river of blood falling into the 8th Circle of Hell.

115. The monastery of Bosco ai Frati, built in the 15th century on designs by Michelozzo.

116. Giambologna: The Appennine Fountain in the park of Villa Demidoff at Pratolino (Florence).

117. The Emperor's Castle at Prato.

118. *The Cathedral and belltower of Prato, with Donatello's pulpit.*

119. *The Chapel of the Holy Girdle, with frescoes by Agnolo Gaddi and assistants. Prato, Cathedral.*

120. *Donatello: Pulpit, detail. Prato, Cathedral.*

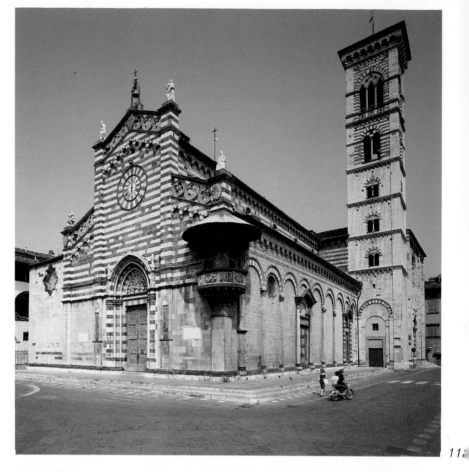

118

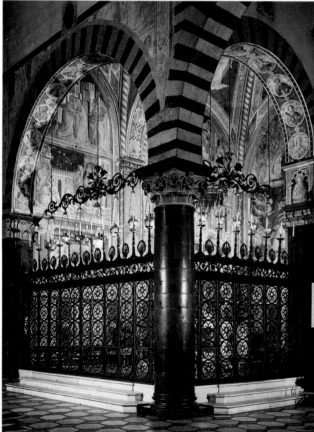

119

120

THE "NUCLEUS" OF TUSCANY

121. The monastery of San Vivaldo, near Montaione (Florence).

We have travelled all the principal roads entering Tuscany across the Appennines from the north-west to the north-east, approaching that "heart" of the region contained by a very irregular triangle with its base on the seashore of Pisa and Versilia and angles at the cities of Viareggio, Livorno and Florence. It is on this core that the system of motorways converges, together with the "superstrade" connecting the "capital" with the industrial and maritime city of Livorno and the residential area of Versilia, while along its irregular sides we find the principal and most active towns in Tuscany: Lucca, Pistoia and Prato, linked by the Firenze-Mare motorway, and Pontedera, Santa Croce sull'Arno and Empoli along the historic and in some ways glorious road down the left hand side of the Lower Arno, the "Tosco-Romagnola", soon to be more or less replaced by the "superstrada" (under construction) for Livorno.

This heart of Tuscany was once a watery place, dotted all over with marshes, grooved by canals (some of which are still there), and travelled by barges and lighters. Once past the crest of Monte Albano, which runs south-east from Serravalle (half way between Pistoia and Montecatini) to meet the Arno near Capraia, and Montelupo right opposite it, above the meeting of the Pesa and the Arno, we reach what was once the great marsh between the Pescia and the Arno, stretching west as far as the Monte Pisano. Now there are only a few watery stretches — pathetic but still beautiful — near Fucecchio and Bientina. It was an area of waterways, which even the reclaiming schemes carried out under Pietro Leopoldo left as they were, because transport by barge was cheaper and safer than road transport. The place-names are often reminders of this ancient land of waters. We need only mention Altopascio, the "High Pass" where the great bell of the monks Hospitaller, known as "La Smarrita" (the Lost One) would ring out to guide travellers wandering on the heath. Or we might think of Scala (port of call), or Isola (island) between Empoli and the ancient administrative centre and imperial stronghold of San Miniato. These names are derived from docks and customs posts. If we come from Florence, once past Lastra and Signa, the eye is caught by the pools of the Gonfolina, mentioned by Leonardo da Vinci, but they are the remnants of a landscape that no longer exists. Between the Autostrada Firenze-Mare and the lower Valdarno today we have the most densely populated zone of Tuscany, and alas the one in which the countryside has been most spoilt and where the environment is most polluted. It is the area devoted to industry, the "islands" of the leather trade, furniture and so on. Here more than elsewhere the traveller should keep a firm hold on the thread of memory and history. In monuments and settlements still wholly or partly intact, in ancient routes now "gutted" by super-highways, and in the place-names, he will in this way be able to find traces of a past that will continue to exist just as long as we go on being able to discern its remains.

122

123

12

122. Detail of the external decoration of
the church of San Giovanni Fuorcivitas,
Pistoia.

123. Pieve di Santa Maria at Cascina.

124. The Collegiate church at Empoli.

125, 126, 127. The facade of the Ospedale del Ceppo in Pistoia is decorated with reliefs by Della Robbia showing acts of mercy. From above: Visiting the Sick, Visiting Prisoners, Burying the Dead.

128, 129. The silver altar of Saint James, in the Cathedral of Pistoia. The central relief showing Saint James (128) by Gilio Pisano and two stories from his life (129) by Leonardo di Giovanni.

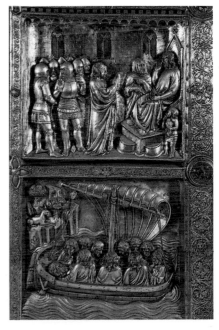

131

132

131. Duccio di Buoninsegna: Maestà. Siena, Cathedral Museum.

132. Simone Martini (attr.to): Guidoriccio da Fogliano. Siena, Palazzo Pubblico.

133. Sandro Botticelli: Primavera (Allegory of Spring). Florence, Uffizi.

134. Piero della Francesca: The Queen of Sheba in adoration of the wood of the True Cross. Arezzo, San Francesco.

"industrial miracle," along with Biella and Reggio Emilia the city with the highest per capita income in Italy?

However, there is no answer to all these questions. Every town, whether it be one's birthplace or somewhere else, answers to a secret code, a spiritual gesture, a unique page in the book of life. One can know every stone of it, or never have seen it except through the medium of pictures and films, of words one has read or heard. A city resembles nothing but itself, and very often this changes from one visit to another. For this reason there are cities I will never tire of seeing, and others (equally dear to my heart) that I never wish to clap eyes on again.

133

134

Wine and Oil

The moment you say Tuscan wine you have said "Chianti." Seeing that the hilly area of Chianti between Siena, Florence and the Valdarno is a pocket handkerchief, it is rather hard to see how so much Chianti of "*Dénomination d'origine controlée*" is at large in the world. But fear not: the good Chianti, the real Chianti, is still there. How does one recognize it? Well, in the first place, of course, by the certified label with a black cockerel on a gold disk. But even more important is to know one's stuff. As with mushroom hunting, the first rule is to be competent.

Wine has a lot of serious and almost religious devotees, and it also has its own history. In Florence, the economic historian Federigo Melis was a great expert on it, and described it in studies which are still famous. But if Tuscan wine was famous even in the Middle Ages, Chianti Classico as it is today is a relatively new product. The historic, mediaeval area of Chianti consists of the three communes of Radda, Gaiole and Castellina, but the "classic" wine-producing zone was more than doubled in 1933, bringing in the communes of Greve, and small parts of those of Castelnuovo Berardenga, Tavarnelle Val di Pesa, Barberino Val d'Elsa and even a few hectares in Poggibonsi. But the area remains extremely small.

Baron Bettino Ricasoli, an austere landowner of the region, a Christian with a streak of Jansenism in him and a leading statesman, laid down the proportions of various kinds of grapes to be used in the making of Chianti Classico. These proportions have been changed somewhat, but still involve a majority (65-70%) of Sangiovese (to give the wine body and colour), some 10 or 15% of Canaiolo to give it softness and aroma. The remainder is made up of two white varieties of grapes, the Trebbiano Bianco and the Malvasia, which give it "finesse" and a touch of acidity (needed for aging). But there are other great wines, with different histories. These are the Brunello di Montalcino, the Vino Nobile di Montepulciano, and the strong, sweet wines from Elba. Other lesser wines, but still excellent, are the "Chianti" from the hills of Siena and Arezzo, that of Val di Sieve (Rufina,

I

II

III

Pomino, Nipozzano), and the wine of the Lower Valdarno (Montalbano, Carmignano).

Less appreciated are the white wines, though they include fine products such as the "virgin" white wines of the Val di Chiana, the gilded Vernaccia of San Gimignano, and the brandnew "Galestro," which appeals to the modern palate because of its light fresh taste and slight effervescence. There are also good dessert wines, "passiti" (made from dried grapes), Muscatel and Vin Santo. In the last few years leading wine producers such as Antinori and Frescobaldi have begun to make a dry sparkling wine by the méthode champenoise, and with considerable success.

The question of olive oil is a more tricky one. The Tuscans consider the famous oil from Liguria to be too thin, and the oil from Puglia, on the contrary, to be too dense and heavy. Until a year or two ago the oils from Lucca were very much appreciated. They are light, and golden, and full of flavour. In these times of "natural" flavours, perhaps people will prefer the heavier oil from Chianti or round Siena, which (when fresh) is green and peppery. But the great freeze-up of February 1985, which killed an overwhelming proportion of the olive trees in Tuscany, may have compromised everything. By now Tuscan oil commands very high prices and we may have to look kindly on coarser oil from Spain, Greece, Turkey or Cyprus. . . and even Puglia.

IV

V

VI

I-II. *Two of the grapes used for making Chianti wine: Sangiovese and Trebbiano.*

III. *The pressing of the grapes.*

IV. *Olive tree pruning.*

V. *The olive harvest.*

VI. *Grapes being dried in order to make "passito" wine and Vin Santo.*

VII. *The Enoteca at Greve in Chianti.*

VII

135

136

135. *The mountain pass of Consuma.*

136. *The forest of Camaldoli.*

FROM FLORENCE TO AREZZO
THROUGH THE CASENTINO

So one leaves Florence, and where does one go? I myself was born and bred on the south bank of the Arno, in the district of San Frediano, so for me the quickest way out would be Porta Romana and then the so-called "Via Senese" out past the Certosa (Charterhouse). From there on we either take the "Volterrana", which cuts across Valdipesa and Valdelsa, or else aim southwards towards Poggibonsi. Here we join the route of the old Via Francigena as far as Siena (though now, alas, everyone roars down the "superstrada"). Coming from Florence, Volterra could well be the springboard for discovering the Maremma, while Siena would fulfil the same function for the Grossetano and the region of Monte Amiata. The fact is, however, that when I was a lad in the mid-Fifties very few young people were lucky enough to have anything grander than a bicycle; and in any case, as far as I was concerned, I was a lone camper, given to taking buses and then getting around on foot. So for me the question of "getting out of Florence" meant taking a bus as far as Pontassieve, so one sees that the journey eastwards was the one I enjoyed most. Then there came a wondrous climb up S.S. 70, which in fact I still know every bend of, and every yard of wall. And up and up I went through places with magical names (Diacceto, Fonte all'Orso) until I reached the Passo della Consuma, the gateway to the Pratomagno. After that I might take the road south through the firwoods as far as Vallombrosa and its great monastery, its vivarium and its tame deer, up to the barren Secchieta that rises to over 1300 metres, and then come down through Saltino and Reggello into the upper Arno valley. Or I could go on (still on S.S. 70) past Romena with the ruins of its castle and its abbey, towards Castel

San Niccolò and Strada, with the road running alongside the plain of Campaldino before arriving at Poppi and Bibbiena. When I was at school, to read Dante was to find myself climbing those roads again, breathing the resinous air of those woods, drinking the icy water of those springs. I well knew the castle of the Counts of Romena, where Maestro Adamo was persuaded to falsify the coinage, thus earning a truly uncomfortable place in hell. I had explored the banks of the Archiano where Buonconte di Montefeltro met his end (Purgatorio V), and was by no means unacquainted with the storms that arise so suddenly in those parts (according to Dante the Devil raised a furious storm, such was his anger at being cheated of Buonconte's soul. . .). I learnt to love old tales from *Novelle della Nonna* (Grandmother's Tales) by Emma Perodi, a sort of Casentino equivalent of the brothers Grimm.

Anyway, this road (S.S. 70) is truly the gateway to the world of wonders. After Castel San Niccolò and before reaching Poppi (coming from Florence) we turn sharp left for Pratovecchio, for Stia, for the incredible fortress of Porciano near which, so legend has it, there lies buried a golden bell that is worth the rest of the Casentino put together. From there we may continue along a road of fearful beauty as far as the Passo della Calla, where it crosses into Romagna, or turn towards Monte Falterona and the source of the Arno. Otherwise, from Poppi it is easy to reach the hermitage of Camaldoli, in the midst of solemn forests, and from there go on to Badia Prataglia and the Passo dei Mandrioli, a few kilometers from Bagno di Romagna. Or yet again — and this is the route I particularly think of as "mine" — from Bibbiena along S.S. 208 to the Franciscan sanctuary of La Verna, the mountain where St. Francis received the stigmata, from which a steep climb through the forest takes one to the peak called "La Penna" at 1283 metres. From here we can gaze upon the Appennines and over Romagna, with Monte Falterona on one side and on the other

137. The apse of the Pieve di San Pietro at Romena.

138. The castle of the Guidi Counts at Poppi.

139. Stradano: View of Vallombrosa in the 17th century. Prato, Villa Pazzi.

140

141

140. *The church of San Salvatore at Ca-maldoli.*

141. *The church of Santa Maria degli Angeli at La Verna.*

142. *Piazza Grande or main square, Arezzo.*

143. *The facade of Santa Maria delle Grazie, Arezzo.*

144. *Overall view of the frescoes by Piero della Francesca and the Crucifix attributed to Margarito d'Arezzo. Arezzo, San Francesco.*

Monte Fumaiolo, source of the Tiber.

Such is the Casentino: technically the region of the high reaches of the Arno, including the Alpe di Catenaia and stretching as far as the threshold of Arezzo and the edge of the Tiber valley. But for me it is the place most belovèd of my soul, containing all the scents and flavours of my childhood and boyhood, the age at which choices and preferences are established for ever, and never change. And — since we know that only fools imagine that history is not made up of ifs and buts — I am perfectly certain that if I had been born a little further from the mountain of St. Francis, or the river of Buonconte da Montefeltro, my whole life would have been quite different.

Tuscan Cooking

Fabio Picchi is the patron of the "Il Cibreo" restaurant in Florence, where they make traditional Tuscan dishes based on research but are not entirely against innovation and even certain cautious but sprightly inventions. But he is absolutely categorical on a number of points. Above all, he serves no pasta whatsoever. In his restaurant the first courses are all soup, both thick and thin, or "pappa" (almost a porridge of bread and vegetables, a fine old Tuscan peasant dish). And indeed he is right. Pasta and risotto were latecomers to Tuscan cooking, and have always remained somewhat clumsily in the sidelines, even if they now take part in a national gastronomic fad that includes such shameful stuff as pasta with caviare or salmon.

Tuscan cooking relies on a handful of down-to-earth things, a lot of myths, and all too many commonplaces. It is a gross error to judge by the scant imagination of the Florentines, who apart from roast spiced pork (arista), fagioli al fiasco (beans cooked in a wine-flask) and castagnaccio (chestnut-flour cake, which in any case comes from the mountains), have invented nothing at all. The beefsteak "alla fiorentina" is more English than Florentine, and requires the meat of the cattle of Val di Chiana. Truly Florentine is "zuppa inglese" (trifle), a ghastly sweet mess evidently made for discontented spinsters. Unless we wish to take shelter behind the delights available in the slums of San Lorenzo, Sant'Ambrogio and the Porcellino, simple boiled tripe and other offal are fighting a rearguard action, while (alas!) the wonderful fried-food vendors of days gone by — now fallen to the level of running a "tavola calda" or prostituting themselves selling sandwiches, have almost entirely forgotten their fried gnocchi made of maize flour, and absolutely forgotten the "roventini" (pancakes made of pig's blood, eaten folded in half inside a round roll) and the "pattona", a kind of polenta made of chestnut flour, sliced with a cheese-wire and eaten boiling hot.

But Tuscan cooking, where for meat and fish the spit and the grill are king, can boast an infinite variety of local dishes. "Cacciucco" (fish soup) is now found all up and down the coast, but was originally from Livorno and is a speciality typical of that "free port", with all its bits and pieces of fish made into a piquant stew served on a base of brown bread.

Among the main dishes, the rather monotonous series of roast meats is now very much à la mode because it is considered more healthy, more "natural" and less high in cholesterol. But what are we to say of the many, all too many restaurants which push their lack of imagination so far as to offer a more or less various dish called "arrosto misto"? This is a dish of extremely modest origins put together in the kitchens of aristocratic homes from the scraps of roast meats left over by the masters, who had themselves nibbled away at them with discretion, one at a time, and in a designated order.

Certainly it is a poor man's table, and often frugal. Sometimes it seems designed for people in a hurry. But poverty and haste are not always allies. On the contrary, there are poor people's foods over which the most extraordinary care is taken. One need

only think of the Sienese "acquacotta", a modest soup based on bread, broth, herbs and fresh eggs. It seems like a mere nothing. Or there is the great and glorious "carabaccia" the onion soup which is the ancestor of the French "soup à l'oignon" (or at least appears to be so). Red onions sliced fine, of course, and an earthenware pot... a little chopped carrot and celery... half a glass of good olive oil, plus salt and pepper. Cook on a slow fire, stir gently but often, then add the broth. Then pour onto slices of toast and add pecorino. That's all there is to it. It is a poor man's cookery, invented by people who had to earn their bread, knew how much things cost and how much sweat it took to make them grow, and who therefore loved and cherished them.

We should also mention the long series of stews and dishes of various kinds of offal that are the pride of the zone of Pistoia. But from Siena down into the Maremma the main attraction is either fresh meat or highly aromatized salami or the truly noble sweetsour wild-boar, with raisins, pine-nuts, a touch of vinegar, and a carefully calculated ration of dark, bitter chocolate.

What about cakes and sweetmeats? In the vanguard come the "panforte" and "ricciarelli" of Siena, both of them inspired inventions. But another of the joys of living, when you can find them, are the "necci" of the Garfagnana. They are thin sheets of pastry made with chestnut-flour and stuffed with the most delicately-flavoured ricotta. It is hard to find them really well made, but when you do, my friend, I tell you it is a treat.

I. Giovanna Garzoni (1600-1670): The Man from Artimino. Florence, Pitti Palace.

II. Jacopo Chimenti called Empoli (1551-1640): Still Life. Florence, Uffizi.

III. The ingredients for a typical Tuscan picnic: prosciutto (cured ham), finocchiona (fennel-flavoured salami), sausages preserved in olive oil, pecorino (sheep cheese) and red wine.

IV. A fruit and vegetable stall at the market of San Lorenzo, Florence.

145

146

145. *The church and tower of Gargonza* *(Arezzo).*

146. *Piero della Francesca: Madonna del* *Parto, detail. Monterchi (Arezzo).*

147. *Piero della Francesca: Resurrection.* *San Sepolcro (Arezzo), Civic Museum.*

VALTIBERINA AND VALDICHIANA

There are several ways of getting to Arezzo. Of course there is the Autostrada del Sole, which passes through the Valdarno and (from Incisa on) runs parallel to S.S. 69. This latter route is far more advisable for anyone who has the time or the wish to look around the upper Valdarno, where the river is cleaner and — between Levane and Ponte a Buriano — is inclined to dawdle in twists and turns and pools. Or you can get to Arezzo by the splendid S.S. 70, which also (after Bibbiena) follows the higher reaches of the Arno.

The "Aretino," or area of Arezzo, is usually underrated by travellers in Tuscany. They pay visits to Arezzo itself, and perhaps Anghiari, Monterchi and San Sepolcro on account of Piero della Francesca, but rarely venture east of the "superstrada" that crosses the Val Tiberina on its way over from Ravenna. In other words no one ever goes to that extraordinary enclave of Tuscany overlooked by the Alpe della Luna and wedged in between Romagna, the Marche and Umbria. This is a real "borderland" which provides a meeting-place for the Florentine "pietra serena," the red brick of Umbria, and the pale pink or pinky-grey brick of Romagna and the Marche. It is a region where the harshness of the Appennines, as well as the cuisine, already has the flavour of the Adriatic.

Certainly, setting out from Arezzo, the tourist less accustomed to leaving the beaten track, or more short of time, might be more attracted southwards, towards the (now reclaimed) lands of the Valdichiana, of Castiglion Fiorentino, and above all the beautiful, mystical town of Cortona, from where he will have a unique view over Lake Trasimeno, and over the southern Sienese lands as far as the hills of Sinalunga, Torrita and Chianciano. In Cortona he will visit the Palazzo Comunale, the Palazzo Pretorio, the Etruscan Museum, the Duomo and the Diocesan Museum which has Fra Angelico's Annunciation. If he has any breath left in his body he will clamber up to the high town, and the acropolis now occupied by the neo-Gothic sanctuary of Santa Margherita.

Not far from the town he will admire the abbey of Farneta, partly ruined; dating from the 9th-10th centuries, this is the oldest early Romanesque church in the Aretino, while its crypt is one of the most incredible in the whole of Christendom. But before getting to Cortona and immersing himself in its wonders, our traveller will have done well to spare at least a glance at Castiglion Fiorentino (well-preserved mediaeval centre, with some interesting Renaissance buildings), and at the castle of Montecchio Vespone, once the feudal property of the 14th-century English military adventurer ("condottiero") Sir John Hawkwood, known in Italy as Giovanni Acuto. If our traveller is a crafty one he will be led to suspect that it is just a trifle too mediaeval to be true, with all those battlements and turrets. It could have been copied from a fresco by Lorenzetti, and yet... this time it is not a neo-Gothic folly.

148

149

150

THE VOLTERRANO AND THE COAST

From Cortona and the Valdichiana one might be tempted to make one's way towards the Valdorcia, Monte Amiata and even Siena. Historically speaking, this would be a plausible itinerary, for Arezzo and Siena fought until the late Middle Ages (first battles of words over the borders of dioceses, and then good hearty stuff with swords) to establish their respective areas of influence in this zone, where there is a strong flavour of nearby Umbria and northern Lazio. But "official" history and tourist brochures gang up lawlessly to link the name of Siena with that of Florence, and with their two bones of contention, Valdelsa and Chianti. And we intend to follow their example.

But not before turning our eyes yet again to the south-west, if we start out from Florence. I am a Florentine who lives on the Porta Romana side of the city, and I often have to go to Siena. Well sometimes, when I get to Galluzzo, I take the right fork at the signpost for Volterra and the detour along the fierce bends of the Gore (nightmare of the amateur cyclists of the "Tour of Tuscany"). Even leaving aside its memories of the Etruscans, and indeed of Gabriele d'Annunzio, Volterra is one of the most beautiful cities in the whole of Tuscany, and this road is the most superb way of getting there.

As usual, of course, there is the short cut for the tourist in a hurry. From Florence one can take the "superstrada" for Siena and pull off at Colle Valdelsa (the upper town of which is well worth a leisurely visit) and then take S.S. 68. Along this we might think of making a few stops or detours, for example at the 15th-century church of Santa Maria delle Grazie, at Casole d'Elsa, at Mensano (with its fine church of San Giovanni Battista), at Radicondoli, and at San Donato di San Gimignano, with its 11th-12th century Romanesque parish church. The road then rises to Volterra, and on its way down offers an extraordinary panorama of cliffs and eroded steeps all the way to the sea.

148. *Fra Angelico: Annunciation and Expulsion from Earthly Paradise. Cortona, Diocesan Museum.*

149. *Francesco Signorelli: Madonna and Saints, detail of the city of Cortona. Cortona, Museum of the Etruscan Academy.*

150. *The cliffs of Volterra.*

151

151. *The cliffs of Volterra with the small church of San Giusto.*

152. *Palazzo dei Priori in the centre of Volterra.*

15

Dominated by the vast bulk of its fortress, Volterra boasts a number of fine mediaeval monuments, such as the Palazzo dei Priori, the Duomo, the Baptistery, the 13th-century church of San Francesco, and many "tower-houses" of the kind so characteristic of the factious family rivalries of the Middle Ages. There are also Roman remains such as the Baths and the Theatre, and the Guarnacci Museum with its famous collection of Etruscan artefacts.

Once we reach Saline di Volterra we may take various roads towards the coast. The most direct is certainly S.S. 68, which follows the valley of the Cècina and after a few dozen kilometers leads to the town of that name at the mouth of the river. It is a seaside resort of some importance, immediately south of the cliffs of the Livornese, with its rocky coast and the beaches (once fashionable) of Calafuria, Quercianella and Castiglioncello. The sandy coast to the south of Castiglioncello, where we find Vada, Cècina itself, Bibbona, San Vincenzo and Riva degli Etruschi, is perhaps a little less sought-after, and in the last few years has lost much of its wild "Maremma" quality. All the same, the road that forks left from S.S. 68 at Ponteginori, and joins the Via Aurelia after the town of Bibbona (with its sanctuary dedicated to the

53

54

155

153. *The fortress of Volterra.*

154. *Etruscan urn called the Urn of Actaeon. Volterra, Guarnacci Museum.*

155. *Rosso Fiorentino: Deposition. Volterra, Pinacoteca.*

Virgin) still retains a certain rough-hewn charm. But it would be wiser to turn south after Saline di Volterra and follow the windy S.S. 439 to Follonica, the seaside resort in the exact centre of the gulf named after it, which ends with the two promontories of Piombino to the north and Punta Ala to the south. This S.S. 439 is a bit of a grind to drive, but is lovely, and will take the traveller through the Colline Metallifere with their woods and their mines (some of which are still working) and the towns of Pomarance with its Etruscan associations and Larderello with its borax-bearing fumaroles. Shortly before reaching the coast, in a landscape full of folds and wrinkles, we come to Massa Marittima, with a splendid Romanesque cathedral set in an irregularly-shaped piazza that creates an impressive scenario. This town, which has a wealth of mediaeval associations, is the "historic capital" of the

156.

15

157

156. *The Palazzo Comunale, or town hall, at Massa Marittima.*

157. *The facade of the church of San Giusto, Suvereto.*

158. *The lower part of the facade of the Cathedral of Massa Marittima.*

Tuscan mining zone. But if our traveller, on arriving in the heart of the Colline Metallifere, should discover that he is panting to get to the sea, then he can turn right after Lardarello and reach the Tyrrhenian at Castagneto Carducci, skirting the hills and pinewoods that once belonged to the noble Pisan Gherardesca clan and (if he has had an Italian education) sipping at memories of the poet Carducci, who celebrated a Maremma that perhaps no longer exists.

Another way of getting to Follonica from Colle Valdelsa, or even from Siena, is to pass through the valley of the Merse. This river, which rises in the Colline Metallifere not far from Montieri, joins the right hand side of the Ombrone after a truly tortuous course through a landscape that is sometimes barren, sometimes gladdened with evergreen scrub and fields of wheat. From Colle we come by way of S.S. 541, which follows the river Elsa for a while and then turns south as far as Le Cetine. From there, bearing right in a south-westerly direction, we get to the impressive Gothic ruins of the Abbey of San Galgano and the nearby chapel of Montesiepi, where one can see the sword which (according to the legend) this saint thrust into a rock at the moment of his conversion. From San Galgano we may take the route via Prata (S.S. 441) to Massa Marittima, or else continue south towards Grosseto through Roccastrada and Montepescali. Rather grim towns, these, closed in on themselves in a barren, isolated landscape. They have an air of southern Italy, and few of those scattered farms and tiny villages that go to make up what we think of as the "classic" landscape of Tuscany.

These are the roads that lead to the coast, and inevitably "flow" at various points into the Via Aurelia. Here, at least if we are south of the Piombino promontory, we breath the aroma of what is left of the Maremma, in the "oases" created by the "nature parks" of Punta Ala (hard-pressed by tourism and the building it brings with it), of the Monti dell'Uccellina, the lagoon of Orbetello that links the coastline to Monte Argentario, and the Lago di

160

9

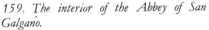

161

Burano which is the last protected remnant of the ancient marshes, and the borderland between the Maremma of Tuscany and of Lazio. In the Maremma there is a hard, bitter quarrel going on between tourism and nature, suspended as it were between open warfare and symbiosis; but it does seem that in the last few years the tourist trade has become more aware and the property speculators more mature, so that they realize that the "development" of the Tyrrhenian shoreline also means the preservation of nature (pinewoods, wild boar and cowboys included), rather than their destruction or systematic reduction in size in order to create a profitable trade in nostalgic memories.

From Livorno there are ferries to Gorgona, Capraia and Elba. From Piombino they run to Elba whence (from Porto Azzurro) we can also reach Pianosa. Boats run from Porto Santo Stefano to Giglio and Giannutri. There are no services to the uninhabited "Formiche di Grosseto," which lie out to sea opposite the Monti dell'Uccellina, and none for Montecristo, which has been made into a Nature Reserve. It is indeed a pleasure to make a cruise through that world of islands in the Tuscan archipelago. It is a world of light, an archaic world, suspended between the fine wines of Elba and the water-shortage in Giannutri, and in which the Mediterranean still seems intact, and clean, glorying in a light and colour that are still "Homeric."

159. The interior of the Abbey of San Galgano.

160. San Galgano drives his sword into the rock. Illustration from a "Biccherna" manuscript, Siena, State Archive.

161. The sword in the rock, in the chapel of Montesiepi near the Abbey of San Galgano.

162

163

162. Terracing and vineyards on the island of Elba.

163. An artisan making baskets, Elba.

164. View of Marciana Marina, Elba.

165. The harbour of Porto, on the island of Giglio.

166. The coast of the island of Capraia.

168

167. *Vineyards and farmers' houses near Greve in Chianti.*

168. *An olive grove near Giogoli (Florence).*

7

THE VALDELSA AND CHIANTI

North of Volterra, and immediately west of the famous Valdelsa, there is a Tuscany in a "minor key" that is rather off the beaten track. It is more or less the area of the roughly parallel valleys of the Egola and the Era, both of them left-hand tributaries of the Arno, joining it respectively at Santa Croce sull'Arno and Pontedera. One can claim that nowadays the part of the Valdelsa north of Poggibonsi is rather neglected as well. From Ponte a Elsa, immediately south-west of Empoli, and Poggibonsi runs the route of the S.S. 429, which brushes that of the ancient Via Francigena; but not many tourists take it. Of the towns it runs through, Certaldo is something of a tourist centre, being the birthplace of Giovanni Boccaccio, while Castelfiorentino is scarcely visited at all. Empoli itself deserves a special mention if only as a kind of Tuscan "mini-Parma," a centre for music-lovers and inveterate Verdi fans. But to the south of Empoli and San Miniato there are a mass of places worth visiting. Lovely Montespertoli, for example, or Gambassi with the nearby Pieve a Chianni, Montaione with its monastery of San Vivaldo near which in the 15th and 16th centuries the Franciscans built a kind of "Holy Mountain" based on the idea of Jerusalem. There is also the area between Peccioli and Castelfalfi, where the countryside is almost untouched, suspended between the raw landscape of the Volterrano and the essence of the Pisan seacoast. This last effect is given by the Maritime Pines, which grow here although we are still some way from the the sea.

The spread of the suburbs and the tendency to take the most "direct" routes to places has in effect made both Tuscans and

169

17

170

172a

169. The castle of Montefioralle (Greve).

170. Badia a Coltibuono.

171. The main square of Greve in Chianti.

172a-b. The walls and the Porta Senese, or gateway leading to Siena, at Monteriggioni (Siena).

17

74

175

73

tourists deaf to the appeal of small towns just outside the city, to the local fairs, which at one time were picnic spots. The Florentines of today no longer go to San Martin la Palma, to Pieve a Giogoli, to San Casciano in Val di Pesa (where — at Sant'Andrea in Percussina — they will find the house where Niccolò Machiavelli lived in exile). Nor do they often visit Impruneta, which for centuries on end was the most famous Marian shrine in the whole of Tuscany. From here, we reach the Valdelsa at Poggibonsi, with its Medici castle above it, and the Franciscan monastery of San Lucchese. People usually leave the superstrada at this point to visit the towers and churches of San Gimignano. This is indeed worth doing, but it is easy to forget that in the immediate neighbourhood there is the lovely Pieve of Cellole and a fascinating mediaeval "Pompeii," by which we mean the incredible sprawling ruins of Castelvecchio, now almost entirely overgrown.

But a traveller who does not wish to get to Siena by the superstrada, can still take the S.S. 222, which leads into the Chianti hills through Greve and Castellina. Or at a certain point (shortly after Panzano) he could fork left into more rugged landscape, to Radda, Gaiole, the Badia a Coltibuono, and the ruins of the Castle of Montegrossi, the original home of the powerful feudal family of the Ricasoli. Here we find ourselves on the watershed of the range of the Chianti hills (which incidentally rise to some 3000 feet). Descending into the Valdarno towards the east, we find the important towns of Figline, San Giovanni and Montevarchi.

173. A typical view of the Chianti country-side, near Badesse (Siena).

174. The church of Saints Cassiano and Ippolito at Badia a Conéo, near Colle Valdelsa.

175. The church of Saints Salvatore and Cirino at Badia a Isola, near Monteriggioni.

176

177

178

176. *San Gimignano.*

177. *Piazza della Cisterna, the main square of San Gimignano.*

178. *The mediaeval towers of San Gimignano.*

179. *Taddeo di Bartolo: Saint Gimignano, patron of the city. San Gimignano, Palazzo del Popolo.*

The Palio of Siena

There is an abundance of festas and contests in costume, as they say in Tuscany (i.e. in mediaeval dress), and some of them are fair enough. Let us avert our gaze from the football game in Florence, which dates back to the 16th century but has a rather spurious background and has never been a great hit with the citizenry. But other such occasions with a serious historical background and an impressive impact are the "Giostra del Saracino" at Arezzo, the "Giostra dell'Orso" at Pistoia, the "Gioco del Ponte" at Pisa, and a number of competitions in crossbow shooting between towns ranging from Massa Marittima to Borgo San Sepolcro.

But nothing, nothing at all, can be compared with the Palio of Siena, in which the entire life of the city comes together. The saying is that "The Palio goes on all year round," and the various sections into which the city is divided work tirelessly year in year out, investing capital, imagination and passion into this event.

As it is at the moment the Palio is run twice a year, on July 2nd (day of the Madonna di Provenzano) and August 16th, the day after the Assumption. In all the other towns in Italy the 2nd of July is one of the first days of the summer holidays, and the 16th is the day after the most important holiday of the year, known in Italy as Ferragosto. The towns and cities are empty. But Siena is cram-full, and feverish with excitement. The race itself consists of three times round the Piazza del Campo by horses representing 10 of the 17 "contrade" (sections) into which the Sienese split up according to birthplace. The jockeys ride bareback and anything goes (e.g. they can knock each other flying or whip each other in the face). The contestants are the seven "contrade" excluded from the previous Palio plus three others drawn by lot. The atmosphere just before the start is so dense it could be cut with a knife, and during the brief moments of the race itself the Piazza explodes.

The Palio lasts all year round, and it is a purely Sienese business, and strangers are tolerated as long as they create no disturbance. For the most important thing for non-Sienese to understand is that the Palio is intensely serious, the most serious thing there is. Anyone eager to grasp some of the atmosphere surrounding it cannot be content with watching the procession in splendid late mediaeval or renaissance costumes which precedes the race. No, he must arrive at least the day before, be present at the "provaccia" or dress rehearsal, see the blessing of the horses in the parish churches, take part discreetly in the night-watch which goes on all night long to prevent one's adversaries from playing any lowdown dirty tricks, and attempt to understand the mechanisms (which include bribery and corruption) by which they try to get their own "contrada" to win, or at least defeat their traditional enemies. For each "contrada" has its allies, its enemies and its downright antagonists. Then, as he wanders around Siena after the Palio, our visitor will have a chance to hear the full-throated joy of the citizens of the winning "contrada" and the rage of the losers. And the day ends with laughter and celebrations.

Unless one has grown up in the shadow of the Palio from childhood on it is impossible to understand the mechanisms of this "game" that twice a year splits families in half and changes the dearest friendships into ferocious antagonism. It is both the glory and the madness of the Sienese, who are most justifiably proud of it.

I. Part of the procession in front of the Cathedral.

II. Just before the race in Piazza del Campo.

III. The race itself.

IV. The procession.

I

II

III

180

180. The belltower and dome of Siena Cathedral.

IN AND AROUND SIENA

The great centre of the south of Tuscany is Siena. Every country has its southlands, its "southern question," its loyalists and its lovers (unless, as in England, it is the other way round, and there is a "northern question"). From Siena down, the landscape is more harsh and bare, the soil more severe and stinting, the colours darker and less merciful. The network of roads down here has a wider mesh, and the settlements are further apart. We more rarely see those little clusters of houses which "humanize" the landscape of Chianti or the Valdelsa. South of Siena grazing gets the better of farming, while industry is confined to mining. In the Senese the summer is more scorching, the winter is more bitter, and the wind more cutting.

Cor tibi magis Sena pandit, we read inscribed on Porta Camollia, gateway to Siena: "Siena opens her heart even wider to you." This is true, on condition that we manage to find the way in. Because to anyone visiting Siena for the first time the city is a labyrinth surrounding the Piazza del Campo, a spiral of concentric and intersecting streets in which the stranger loses his way at once. Churches and palaces, tower-houses and warehouses all look the same, and if you pass twice in front of the same building there is a risk that you won't recognize it — unless, of course, it happens to be Palazzo Tolomei or Palazzo Salimbeni. Siena changes with the seasons and with the light at different times of day, and its face of pale red brick and brown-gold or iron-grey travertine is always different. It appears warm and welcoming, but it retains something of enigma and mystery, of a hermetic emblem no less hard to interpret than the esoteric symbols inlaid in the floor of its wonderful cathedral.

The Sienese have been this way for centuries: coarse and courageous, proud of their background and given to flights of greatness and of braggartry. In the Middle Ages they lost their battle against the bankers of Florence because they had no gold coinage and because they had backed the wrong horse — the Ghibelline party supporting the Empire. They lost once more, against the wool manufacturers of Florence because they were short of water, which is indispensable in the making of textiles. In exchange for this, they "thought big". Their enormous cathedral dedicated to the Virgin Mary was planned to be merely the transept of another, truly gigantic construction. A shell, or sketch, of what would have been the walls, still looms over the city. They were "people full of vanity" who were thought (Dante, Inferno XXIX) to have introduced the use of the costly clove into their cooking, and who could boast of gangs of gilded youths who amused themselves by quite literally throwing money away (gold florins in this case). Just look at the gorgeous sweetmeats they still know how to make from the finest honey, the most flavourful dried fruits, the most fragrant almond paste. Compare them with the scrawny glory of Florentine confectionery, the flat cake made with a fistful of flour and a powdering of icing sugar. The

181

181. The Cathedral of Siena.

centuries-old rivalry between Siena and Florence can all be summed up in this: it is the clash between the proud generosity and extravagance of the people who created the Piazza del Campo and the suspicious stinginess of the men who created capitalism.

Isolated, defeated and subjugated, Siena has become a wonderful historical fossil, and when it really comes down to it, in the debased Tuscany of today, she is the winner. Go and see the Palio and attempt to understand it. If you do, then you will realize that you have not seen a game, or a festival, but something truly unique in anthropology, the secret and hidden (well, perhaps not so hidden) motive force of a city. In it are the courage, ferocity, pride, thirst for adventure and love of hazard of one of the greatest and most glorious peoples on the face of the earth.

There are two ways of leaving Siena towards the south. One can take S.S. 223, which follows the Merse valley for a while on its way to Civitella, Paganico and the ruins of Roselle (which are worth the short detour involved), and finally arrives in Grosseto. From there we can pay visits to Vetulonia, Castiglion della Pescaia (as stern as a Spanish fortress in the Carribbean), and the lovely

182

182. Pinturicchio: The Meeting of Frederick III and Eleanor of Portugal, detail of the city of Siena. Siena, Cathedral, Piccolomini Library.

183. The inside of the Cathedral with an overall view of the marble floors, Siena.

18

Maremma of Grosseto. I advise a trip to the Uccellina Nature Reserve, and to the ruins of San Rabano to be found there. Otherwise we may take S.S. 2, the Via Cassia. A few miles down this road and we find ourselves in a lunar landscape, with the horizon dominated by the bulk of Monte Amiata. Here we cross the Val d'Arbia and arrive at Buonconvento at the point where this river flows into the Ombrone. The Arbia, incidentally, is the river said by Dante to have been "dyed red" in 1260, when the Sienese Ghibellines defeated the Guelphs of Florence at Montaperti (Inferno X, in the episode of Farinata).

To return to Buonconvento, famous because the emperor Henry VII died there in 1313, the town forms a rectangle surrounded by fine 14th-century walls. From here we advise at least two detours. First and foremost, if we take S.S. 451 in a north-easterly direction we pass through the barren landscape of the "Crete," with its colours that vary from pale grey to ochre to sulphur yellow and finally to the dark "burnt Siena," and arrive at the Abbey of Monte Oliveto Maggiore, the "mother-house" of the Olivetan Order, which was founded in the 14th century by a group of Sienese

184. *Palazzo Pubblico, Siena.*

185. *Palazzo Sansedoni in Piazza del Campo, Siena.*

aristocrats as a reformed branch of the great Benedictine Order. Several times remodelled between the 14th and 19th centuries, dominating the landscape with its impressive red-brick bulk, the monastery still preserves the precious cloister with paintings by Signorelli and Sodoma.

After Monte Oliveto the tourist who likes to see only the essential — and thinks he knows what it is — can turn and retrace his steps and go on down the Via Cassia. His wiser and more patient colleague, however, will not let slip the opportunity of pushing a little further north, as far as Asciano Senese (where he will find a delightful little parish museum containing a 14th century panel of the Madonna that was one of the great loves of my adolescence). Or else he can turn south and follow secondary and justifiably dusty roads (dust forms part of the fascination of the "Crete") as far as Lucignano, a lovely little town on account of its oval shape — typical of what in Tuscany is called a "castle," or in other words a fortified village — and also for the view over the neighbouring Valdichiana and for the magnificent "Albero di San Francesco," the most extraordinary silver-gilt reliquary in the

186

187

186. Sala della Pace, or room of Peace, with the frescoes of the Allegory of Good Government by Ambrogio Lorenzetti. Siena, Palazzo Pubblico.

187. The chapel of San Martino. Siena, Piazza del Campo.

whole art of Siena, or of Italy, and perhaps not only of Italy. . .

We return to Buonconvento and prepare for the second "compulsory" trip. We take another "secondary" road to Montalcino, the last heroic bulwark of Sienese freedom against the tyranny of the Medici, with its fine Palazzo Comunale, its mighty fortress, its superb red wine (Brunello, which can mature and improve for as much as forty years) and its homemade pasta known as "pici". About ten kilometers south of Montalcino we get to the Benedictine abbey of Sant'Antimo, maybe the most beautiful and certainly the most touching of all the Romanesque churches in Tuscany. It is no longer in service, as it were, but luckily still in a good state of preservation. The onyx decorations from the nearby quarries of Castelnuovo give it a uniquely iridescent look. This visit will take as much time as you care to give it, from half a day to weeks on end. About fifteen years ago I happened to camp nearby with a bunch of young friends, and for day after day we never tired of simply gazing at it. Even now, to go back there is to revisit something eternal in one's life, a time of unsullied happiness and a memory that brings only comfort.

But it is time to get back on the Via Cassia, and head south towards the Val d'Orcia. The historic chief town of the valley is San Quirico d'Orcia, in which the tourist who thinks of himself more as a true "traveller" would do well to spend some time; not only to look at it really thoroughly, but to make it his base for two long but exquisite excursions, one to south-eastern Tuscany, the other to the area of Monte Amiata.

188

But San Quirico should not be neglected in itself. In many respects it is a typically "Sienese" town, with its winding streets and brick-built towers with the purest lines. Of special interest is the splendid Romanesque collegiate church (the ancient Pieve di Osenna, dedicated to Saints Quirico and Giulitta), which can boast a genuine masterpiece in its Roman portal decorated with monsters and other figures. There is also the great Palazzo Chigi, a vast building of the late 17th century that appears to have been designed for a city such as Rome, and which here — enormous, isolated, almost frightening — is so disproportionate as to give one a certain enigmatic delight. Finally there are the "Orti Leonini," the large 16th century gardens.

S.S. 146, which heads east from San Quirico d'Orcia, is the best road to take if you want to enjoy the south-east of the "Senese". After 10 kilometers or so you reach Pienza, the model town built in brick and travertine by order of Pope Pius II, who as a member of the family of the local lords (the Piccolomini) was born there. At that time it was called Corsignano, and was only re-named Pienza after him.

As it is today the town can be considered from a number of points of view. One of these is certainly the Utopian Renaissance notion of the "ideal city", with straight streets and perfect proportions, and all based on Neo-Platonic models. But as it is so small it is more of a toy town, the whim of a Humanist overlord who became pope, translated into four streets forming a cross around the serene and perfect piazza, with the cathedral built

189

188. *The Sienese "Crete" (bare, clay hills) near Monte Oliveto.*

189. *Vineyards near Montepulciano.*

190

191

19

19

190. The apse and the belltower of the abbey of Monte Oliveto Maggiore.

191. The 14th-century city walls of Buonconvento.

192. Luca Signorelli: Saint Benedict confirms the rule of the Olivetan Order, detail. Monte Oliveto Maggiore.

193. Erosion furrows near Chiusure.

194. The interior of the Abbey of Sant'Antimo.

according to designs by Bernardo Rossellino, the Palazzo Piccolomini by the same architect (here clearly inspired by Alberti's Palazzo Rucellai in Florence), and the Palazzo Comunale weighed down by restorations carried out in this century. And as a background to the piazza, behind the church, the mass of Monte Amiata completes the scenic effect. A little down from the town the serene and simple Pieve di Corsignano (11th-12th centuries) reminds the visitor of the mediaeval nature of the place. Still travelling east from Pienza we get to Montepulciano, which can boast splendid 14th to 16th century buildings in the town centre, such as the church of Sant'Agostino (by Michelozzo), the late-Renaissance Palazzo Avignonesi (attributed to Vignola) and the 16th-17th century Duomo. The central piazza possesses a rare harmony, even though it is surrounded by buildings from various periods. We need hardly add that it would be madness to leave Pienza without a little store of "pecorino" cheeses, both fresh and

195

196

1

195. *The Collegiate church of Sant'Agata at Asciano (Siena).*

196. *Domenico di Niccolò dei Cori: Angel of the Annunciation. Montalcino, Diocesan Museum.*

197. *The Collegiate church at San Quirico d'Orcia.*

matured, mild or piquant according to taste; or to leave Montepulciano without a reserve of the celebrated local wine, the "Vino Nobile" which — according to Dr. Francesco Redi, physician to the archduke and a great enologist — is "king of all wines."

Enriched by these delights of the palate we continue towards the place where those who enjoy them to excess are fated to end up: Chianciano Terme, a famous hydrotherapeutic centre and a pleasant town, though perhaps too much the watering and holiday place that flourished most brilliantly in the Thirties. Of this it still bears the traces in the Fascist architecture of the public buildings

and the bourgeois taste for little private villas. Our route lies through Chianciano if we want to get to the lovely town of Chiusi, with its mediaeval Duomo (6th-12th centuries, but very much altered in the 12th), the National Etruscan Museum and the Etruscan tombs scattered outside the town. We advise you to take a glimpse at the two lakes of Chiusi and Montepulciano to the north of the necropolis area.

Any one itinerary is debatable. A short while back we crossed the Val di Chiana coming from Arezzo. It would certainly have been logical from there, having visited Cortona with its Etruscan museum and associations, to have reached Chiusi by following the Chiana or else S.S. 71 which runs beside Lake Trasimeno. Another possible choice, and certainly an interesting one, would be to get to Chiusi by striking east-south-east from Siena, which would open up to us more of the Sienese Val di Chiana. Anyone preferring this solution should leave Siena by S.S. 326 or 428, which in any case join up after about thirty kilometers near Rapolano Terme, another of the watering places in the Sienese country that repays a visit. From that point S.S. 326 leads to Sinalunga, a fine town full of art and industry (manufacture of tiles and furniture) and to Torrita, where the brick is redder and the geraniums more magnificent than elsewhere. You see them everywhere, in flower-pots set in iron hoops outside the windows, according to a system common throughout central Italy, but especially flourishing around Siena. And from there a brief detour northwards will bring you to the agricultural centre of Foiano della Chiana. Either by state road or the motorway it is easy to get from Torrita to Chiusi, whence one may head south for Cetona and for the spas of San Casciano.

198. *The parish church at Ancaiano (Siena).*

199. *View of Montalcino.*

200. *Domenico di Niccolò dei Cori: Virgin of the Annunciation. Montalcino, Diocesan Museum.*

201

20

202

201. *The Cathedral of Pienza.*

202. *Etruscan canopic urn. Chiusi, National Museum.*

203. *Palazzo Piccolomini, Pienza.*

204. *View of the town of Sinalunga.*

205. *The church of San Biagio at Montepulciano.*

20

206

206. The church of the Benedictine Abbey of Abbadia San Salvatore.

207. The Aldobrandeschi fortress at Pian Castagnaio.

20

MONTE AMIATA

But let us return to San Quirico d'Orcia, for an itinerary that will take us south-south-west by S.S. 323 and the roads branching off it towards Monte Amiata. From Castel del Piano one easily reaches the summit of the mountain at 1738 metres, with a superb panorama as far as the Tyrrhenian and Lakes Trasimeno and Bolsena. But I advise a proper visit to the whole of the massif, with its lovely chestnut forests and picturesque villages, such as Pian Castagnaio, as well as the summits of Monte Calvo (930 metres) and Monte Civitella (1107 metres). At Abbadia San Salvatore you will find what is left of the famous Benedictine abbey that dates back to the 8th century, and the abbot of which, in the late Middle Ages, was one of the most powerful overlords in the region. The church is Romanesque, but the delightful crypt goes back to the period of its foundation. Another noteworthy Romanesque church is that of Saints Fiora and Lucilla at Santa Fiora. From here we reach Arcidosso, and enter the area of "Lazzarettian" pilgrimages.

This is an interesting story not widely known outside Italy. The "Prophet of Amiata", Davide Lazzaretti, was a carter born in Arcidosso in 1834, and there from 1868 to 1878 he led a religious cult based on asceticism and penitence, and marked by a strong tendency to millenarism (the expectation of "Christ the Leader and Judge"), as well as by generous if somewhat confused social ideals. With his great personal attraction he had a large following among the peasants and shepherds of Monte Amiata. His actions were totally foreign to any sort of violence, and he does not even seem

to have toyed with any Protestant ideas — indeed he had a profound reverence for the Virgin Mary. But he was condemned by the Church and also awakened concern among the civil authorities, who were anxious about social protests and unrest. On August 18th 1878 Lazzaretti, having proclaimed himself the Christ of the Second Coming, came down from his Sacred Mountain, the nearby Monte Labbro (1183 metres) at the head of a harmless procession of his followers. At the entrance to Arcidosso a platoon of Carabinieri mowed them down, killing the "Prophet" and many other innocent people. On the site of this slaughter there is now a neo-Gothic chapel to commemorate this sad act of repression, one of many which the government of newly-united Italy perpetrated in Tuscany and elsewhere. On Monte Labbro, in an enclosure invaded by sheep, there is the modest sanctuary of the "Chiesa Giurisdavidica" founded by Lazzaretti. It is a narrow fissure in a rock. Plenty of followers of the cult remain in the area, and they even have a temple in Rome.

208. *Landscape near Radicofani.*

209. *The cloister of the monastery of Pian Castagnaio.*

210. *The conduit of a fumarole near Pian Castagnaio.*

"Peasant Culture"

Great and small, public and private, museums of "peasant culture" are now quite numerous, though not all of equal quality. We will confine ourselves to mentioning those at San Pellegrino and Villafranca in Val di Magra. There are also quite a number of studies of Tuscan farmhouses (case coloniche) and manor houses. The most reliable approach to the peasant world of Tuscany, once we have set aside a somewhat ambiguous nostalgia for the country, is found in the study of materials and old techniques of labour and production. The Mugello, Alto Valdarno, Valdelsa, Valdorcia and the inland parts of the Maremma are the areas where the traditional style of building held out for longest. Among the more important objects that have fallen into disuse, a notable role is played not so much by work-tools — which, in what in the broad sense is a "pre-industrial" environment, have a very long life and can still come in useful in a minor way — as by the weights and measures for both dry goods and liquids. The abandonment of these led to a real mental "revolution", especially around the time of the unification of Italy.

If it is difficult today to interpret the function of long discarded tools, and to reconstruct ancient methods of production with any degree of certainty, it is still more difficult to reconstruct a mental world connected with living conditions profoundly different from those obtaining today. We have to think of houses without running water or electricity, of the trouble of doing things that today we scarcely think about, of the darkness that plummets down on everything immediately after sunset, the uncertain, dangerous light from the fire, of candles and oil lamps. It was in such a context that people got together and sang songs and told stories, the latter (according to tradition) being either terrifying or magical.

Much of this everyday world can be found today in the oral tradition. There are songs of love, of nostalgia, but also of political passion; there are ancient therapeutic recipes; ballads, satirical verses, traditional open-air performances known as "bruscelli" and so forth; magical formulas and charms. All these are part of a culture made up of proverbs and sayings that seem never to change. From time to time in folk traditions there is an outcrop of ancestral memory, even going back beyond Christian times, as in the various cults in Chianti and the Aretino that have to do with water and with "galactoforous" stones, which help nursing mothers to produce more milk. Then there is the tradition of butchering an ox every year in honour of the Virgin of the Sanctuary of the Madonna del Sasso in Val di Sieci, which it seems occupies the site of an ancient pagan holy place.

This legacy of folklore has in the past been gleaned, but also re-interpreted and in part distorted by writers such as Renato Fucini, Vittorio Imbriani and Emma Perodi. More recently it has been examined with more care by such good anthropologists as Vittorio Dini, Pietro Clemente and Alessandro Falassi, while the songs have been once again re-interpreted by performers with a fine ear for genuine folk-music, such as Caterina Bueno, Alfredo Bianchini and Riccardo Marasco.

I

II

III

V

I. *The courtyard of a typical farmer's house in Tuscany.*

II. *Vines are often supported by trees, in this case mulberries.*

III. *View of the countryside near Arezzo, with different kinds of cultivations in a small space.*

IV. *Giovanni Fattori (1825-1908): Maremma, detail of the oxen pulling a cart. Florence, Gallery of Modern Art.*

V. *Oxen pulling a harrow.*

211

211. *The walls of the fortress of Radico-fani.*

212. *View of the "Crete" near Radico-fani.*

213. *Early morning mist in the valleys near the Pass of Radicofani.*

214. *View of Pitigliano.*

TOWARDS ANCIENT TUSCIA

We return northwards along S.S. 323, visiting Seggiano, Castiglione d'Orcia (with the ruins of the castle of the mightiest feudal family of southern Tuscany, the Aldobrandeschi, lords of Santa Fiora) and Rocca d'Orcia, overlooked by other impressive ruins, those of the fortress at Tintinnano dei Salimbeni. Here we once more join the Via Cassia, which however it is better to leave about fifteen kilometers further south (at Bisarca) to fork left up S.S. 478 to the volcanic rock of Radicofani, a town impressive in its solitude and dominated by a severe 13th century fortress several times rebuilt. At its foot is the 16th century "Palazzo della Posta", a hostel and customs post at the borders of the grand duchy and the Papal States. The pass at Radicofani, mentioned even by Boccaccio on account of the bandit Ghino di Tacco who terrorized it, was for centuries the place at which the Via Francigena left Tuscany.

Present-day administrative boundaries cut across an area that in fact has a deep-seated unity, and that we suggest should be visited, starting from Radicofani and continuing along the Cassia as far as Acquapendente, in the part of Tuscia which falls in Lazio. Here we should see the ancient church containing the late mediaeval votive chapel of the Holy Sepulchre. In this way we shall travel through the whole of the ancient feudal domain of the Farnese family: Grotte di Castro, the west bank of the Lake of Bolsena, Ischia di Castro, Farnese itself, the ruins of the town of Castro, and then — using S.S. 312 — the Etruscan necropolis of Vulci. Continuing south we meet the Via Aurelia at Montalto di Castro, whence after a few kilometers we find ourselves at the marvellous town of Tarquinia; we then go on to Tuscania, with its Etruscan remains and its incomparable mediaeval churches. In a word, what we have is the whole region of "Tuscia in Lazio" contained within a perimeter that follows the Via Cassia to the east of the Lake of Bolsena, touches Montefiascone, arrives at Viterbo, and then at Ventralla from which S.S. 1bis takes us to Tarquinia. Whatever the administrative borders may be, if we do not visit this area we cannot understand southern Tuscany, which is closely united with it in history and landscape, quite apart from the fact that the "Etruscan Itinerary" that we started at Cortona and Chiusi must logically end at Tuscania, Tarquinia and Vulci.

But for our visit to Tuscia we do not have to start from the line of the Cassia. We can also make a perfectly logical tour starting from Orbetello, which stands on the sandbar connecting the Argentario to the mainland. From there the Via Aurelia runs east-south-east past the ruins of the Etruscan city of Cosa above Ansedonia, crosses the reclaimed area of the Lake of Burano and travels on past Montalto di Castro. All the same, shortly after the lake, which we leave on our right because it is wedged in between the coast and the road, we will turn off and head for the pretty little town of Capalbio, with its mediaeval walls and its splendid cuisine typical of the Maremma. Going north from Capalbio we

2

213

214

215

216

2

215. *Vineyards along the cliffs at Sorano.*

216. *The Etruscan-Roman bridge at Vulci.*

217. *The town of Sorano.*

can link up with the Amiata tour we have just described. We will see Manciano, the sulphur baths of Saturnia (which can also be reached easily from Arcidosso and Santa Fiora), and further to the east Sovana, birthplace of Hildebrand, the 11th-century monk who became pope with the name of Gregory VII. It has the ruins of an Aldobrandeschi fortress and some lovely Romanesque churches. Further on, Pitigliano has the immense Orsini castle, and the tufa precipices honey-combed with caves that make one aware how close one is to Lazio. From Sovana a path leads down to an impressive Etruscan necropolis composed of tombs cut into the tufa cliffs, in a precipitous landscape as breath-taking as any in the region.

These are a few, and perhaps all too few, of the multitude of things one can see in Tuscany. I cannot even claim that they are the most important; and in any case, with the aid of guides and maps and asking questions when on the spot, everyone will be able to work out his own itinerary, choosing between what I have mentioned and what I have had to leave out for reasons of space. But this is "my" Tuscany, the Tuscany of my own experiences, and knowledge, memories, tastes and perhaps even

219

220

manias both great and small. I do not so much admire as love this part of the world. Others may want to do things in a different way, and to "pick up" on different things. For my part I have tried to avoid making a museum of a world abounding in beauties and works of art, but one that should be taken as its own rhythms dictate, with an approach as free as is humanly possible, within which a traveller does not feel guilty if he misses a church or omits to visit a palace. The Tuscans are a frugal people, with a fund of antique avarice derived from their historical experiences, which have not always been easy. They are a people who hate surfeit and indigestion of any kind, art and culture included. The intelligent visitor will not gobble down the Romanesque and the Gothic, the hills and the seashores; he will select with care, taste with discretion, and enjoy a little at a time. With luck he will be able to put some things off until next time — for there is always a next time, to come to Tuscany.

218. The facade of the Palazzo dell'Archivio at Sovana.

219. The apse of the Cathedral of Sovana.

220. Etruscan vase. Grosseto, Archeological Museum.

(following pages)
221. The river Fiora near Saturnia.

222. Ignazio Danti (1536-1586): Map of Italy, detail of Tuscany. Vatican, Gallery of Maps.

221

INDEX OF ILLUSTRATIONS